s it be ee?

the Foundation Stage

Published by Step Forward Publishing Limited, 25 Cross Street, Leamington Spa, Warwickshire CV32 4PX
Telephone: 01926 420046   www.practicalpreschool.com
© Step Forward Publishing 2003   Illustrations by Cathy Hughes.

What does it mean to be three? ISBN: 1-902438-88-4

With thanks to Squirrels Nursery, Moseley, Birmingham where the cover photo was taken.

Introduction

The Foundation Stage

In England, the period of early childhood education from three years to five or close to six years is called the Foundation Stage. Children may be in a range of early childhood settings over this time and will start school in the Reception year when they are four or five. The Foundation Stage ends when children enter Year 1 in school, by which time the oldest will be close to their sixth birthday, but the youngest children are still not long past their fifth. It is important to bear in mind that these are still young children in terms of development.

The aim of the Foundation Stage was to create a coherent period for early education that properly acknowledged the learning and continued development of children younger than school age. A broad framework was established for early years practitioners to support children's learning in six areas:

- Personal, Social and Emotional Development
- Communication, Language and Literacy
- Mathematical Development
- Knowledge and Understanding of the World
- Physical Development
- Creative Development

This framework is one way of considering the breadth of children's learning. But, of course, children do not learn in separate compartments; the whole point is that children's learning crosses all the boundaries. The aim of identifying areas of learning is to help adults to create a balance, to address all the different important areas of what children gain in the early years.

Wales, Scotland and Northern Ireland have their own early years curriculum documents and they offer similar, although not identical, divisions to guide support for children's learning. These documents also provide general expectations for what children will manage by the end of the early years period and their entry into school.

In each of the six areas of learning, there are a set of Early Learning Goals that describe what it is hoped will be achieved by most children by the end of the Foundation Stage. The goals are not intended to be used with three-year-olds; they are the end of the journey. The guidance therefore includes ideas for each goal on how younger children might build their skills and understanding. The concept and visual presentation of these stepping stones highlights firmly that children learn along the route to the Early Learning Goals. The pattern is different for individual children and some goals have a less clear developmental pattern.

In order to help practitioners, the Foundation Stage guidance

(Qualifications and Curriculum Authority, 2000) provides three broad areas of information in addition to the Early Learning Goals for each of the six areas of learning. The guidance identifies:

- *Stepping stones* - to help practitioners plan
- *Examples of what children do* – to help practitioners assess
- *What the practitioner needs to do* – to help practitioners teach

These examples work as highlights to support flexible and creative practice. The three kinds of example are not a full statement of all that is possible, nor are they intended to be used as if they are a curriculum in themselves. The stepping stones in each learning area are not the only elements in young children's learning towards that given goal, any more than the examples are the only acceptable ways in which children will show this learning. And, of course, the suggestions for what the practitioner needs to do are not the final and exclusive statement of how adults can help. All of these are examples: to support and not to confine practitioners.

The guidance explains that the stepping stones are provided to help practitioners plan, since they show: '... the knowledge, skills, understanding and attitudes that children need to learn during the Foundation Stage in order to achieve the Early Learning Goals. They are not age-related, although it is likely that three-year-old children will be better described by earlier stepping stones, shown in the yellow band, progressing through those in the blue band, with later stepping stones in the green band normally describing older children in the Foundation Stage. The Early Learning Goals form the final stepping stones.' (*Curriculum Guidance for the Foundation Stage*, page 5)

So the stepping stones and examples of children are descriptions to highlight ways in which three-, four- and five-year-olds might be learning and progressing towards the relevant Early Learning Goal. They were never intended to be subsidiary goals, a developmental check-list, nor an observational tracking system. However, anecdotal evidence suggests that some settings feel they should, or are being required, to treat the stepping stones as if they work as a developmentally tested sequence. This is not the case, so it is inappropriate if settings are required to show evidence that children have 'passed' each stepping stone before they are 'allowed' to move on. This misunderstanding creates weighty, paper-heavy systems in which children are not observed as individuals.

The Foundation Stage guidance stresses how much children need to experience an environment that supports the development of a positive disposition to learn. Children are learning about learning as well as gaining knowledge and skills. Early childhood settings need to support or create positive outlooks on learning so that children are well prepared to continue to learn in their school years. Their Foundation Stage experience needs to enthuse them and help them to feel competent and able to learn; to feel increasingly that they are young learners. Children's future learning and their growing sense of self-esteem can be seriously shaken if their early years experience is over-structured and too formal.

The three linked books, of which this is the first, describe what and how children are learning in the three broad age bands of the Foundation Stage.

- In this book the focus is on three-year-olds and children slightly younger, recognising that at least some playgroups, pre-schools and nursery schools or classes take children in the last six months or so before their third birthday. Their youngest children may therefore be only two and a half years old. They are very young children.

- The second book focuses on four-year-olds, some of whom will be in pre-school settings like nursery or playgroup. But many four-year-olds will have moved into a Reception class.

- The third book is on five-year-olds, all of whom will be within school, some in the Reception class, but the children whose birthday is later in the calendar year will join Year 1 as a young five-year-old.

All the books recognise that children from the age group will be in different kinds of settings and some with childminders. But the objective is to approach them as three-, four- and five-year-old children, rather than only through their role as a child in pre-school or nursery or as a school pupil. The books are organised according to the six learning areas of the Foundation Stage. However, the aim remains to approach learning through child development and children's needs, rather than how children can be made to fit the requirements of a group setting. Children's learning can only be effectively and appropriately supported when adults, practitioners and parents are guided by sound knowledge of child development.

You will find a similar range of material within each book:

- Descriptive developmental information within the main text, organised within the six areas of learning used by the Foundation Stage.
- **For example** sections giving instances of real children and real places.
- **Being a helpful adult** boxes which focus on adult behaviour that is an effective support for children's learning, as well as approaches that can undermine young children.
- **Food for thought** headings which highlight points of good practice in ways that can encourage reflection and discussion among practitioners, as well as sharing in partnership with parents.

The framework for the Foundation Stage aims to create a coherent pattern over these years but for many children it will be a time of change, with perhaps more than one transition. Over the years of the Foundation Stage, some children will have changes of early years provision and the majority will join mainstream school in the Reception year at four or five years of age. Children need to negotiate these changes and they appreciate appropriate adult support. Yet their entry to school is no more the beginning of their learning than their entry to nursery or pre-school. It may be a different kind of learning experience, but no child is starting from a blank sheet in terms of knowledge, skills and attitudes towards the business of learning.

Value children as themselves

Young children need to be and feel valued for what they are at the moment. Their development unfolds because they are encouraged and allowed to relish what they are learning at the moment. Four-year-olds need to have been enabled to enjoy being three-year-olds, five-year-olds need to have spent time being unharassed four-year-olds. Such a

perspective may seem obvious but, unfortunately, the sense of pressure felt by some early years practitioners, and some parents, is that children, even young children have effectively been pushed onto a treadmill, especially an intellectual treadmill. There has been far too much 'getting children ready for…', 'making sure that they can… because…' and a sense that 'children must/have to/ought to..'

The aim of the Foundation Stage should be that children have a full and enjoyable experience of learning. Despite the rhetoric of some educational materials, the aim of the Foundation Stage is not to prepare children for Year 1, then Key Stage 1 and SATS (in England). Some of the most serious problems arise for children when adults take a school model and impose it on younger children, when they misunderstand or ignore the insights from knowledge of child development:

- Children learn from their whole day and not only within the hours or the activities that adults define as 'educational'. Children need and learn a great deal from care, an adult caring orientation and active involvement in daily and weekly care routines.

Food for thought
Young children are important as themselves; they are not pre-anything. For this reason I avoid using the word 'pre-schooler' to refer to children under five years. We do not call adolescents 'pre-workers' or people in their fifties 'pre-retirees'!

Some early years settings are known as pre-schools. Consequently that term for a group is familiar, although by no means all settings choose to use this term. There are some potential problems about defining your group, and therefore your early years curriculum, as 'prior to school'. However, in my view, calling young children themselves 'pre-schoolers' seriously increases the risk that their learning and experiences are valued only as school preparation.

- Children learn a considerable amount from play, but they do not learn only from play and this learning can be seriously curtailed if adults over-structure, over-direct and, frankly, highjack children's play and play activities.

- Children's current learning, and the step-by-step nature of their learning, must be recognised as valuable now. What three- or four-year-olds have learned is not of value just because it will set them up more effectively for school work. Children can sense and are disturbed by adult anxiety and pressure. They begin, sadly, to feel that their current learning is never enough; they will see themselves as always chasing something, never getting there.

- If we want children to be enthusiastic learners and set themselves up as much as possible for the challenges of primary and secondary school, then they must experience generous respect and adult enthusiasm for their current skills and struggles. What children are learning is valuable now, not just because it leads onto something that adults think is more important.

The positive disposition to learn

Children are learning about the business of learning. The outlook that they take on in the years before starting school can establish a firm base of enthusiasm and build strong self-esteem. On the other hand, experiences that disrupt children's confidence, and make them doubt their ability, can seriously undermine their outlook for the school years. Experience within early years settings is also significant for the attitudes that children develop towards key adults outside their family. Do the children begin to believe that adults are there to help and support? Or do they build an image of adults who are more likely to nag, disrupt enjoyable play, make you do apparently pointless tasks and perhaps make you feel as a child that what you produce is never quite good enough?

The importance of children's attitudes is highlighted in the Foundation Stage document for England: 'A positive disposition to learn grows from experiences that children enjoy and can control, are interesting and aid success. Such experiences foster feelings of competence and self-confidence. They motivate children to learn and carry on learning'. (page 29)

Any discussion of early learning has to acknowledge that the individuality of children matters. They learn by making connections to what they already know or half understand. Learning is a personal experience and adult support or guidance can only help with full recognition of individual children. Adults can enable children to learn; you do not make them learn.

Healthy emotional development for young children is supported by a growing belief that they are competent individuals, a sense of 'I can' and that 'I can't yet' is not a disaster, because adults are supposed to help children who are struggling or have made a mistake. Many four- and five-year-olds are beginning to realise that they have a great deal to learn in the future. Children need a positive outlook on themselves as learners if they are not to feel overwhelmed by the prospect of years of having to tackle new learning tasks one after another. They desperately need supportive adults who will tune into realistic expectations for the age group and to individual children's version of being a five-, six- or seven-year-old.

Children's positive disposition to learn includes all of the following:

- Curiosity and the wish to find out and explore;
- A desire to become competent, to be able to do or say something;
- A motivation to keep trying, even if something is neither easy nor obvious at the outset;
- A sense of personal satisfaction for children when they practise, improve and realise that they have managed a new skill or idea.

Enthusiastic and supportive adults help children to develop this positive outlook. Alternatively, children may learn from negative experiences that they are incompetent, that adults think they keep making mistakes and that there is no point in trying, because you are either 'good at something' or 'useless'.

What makes a supportive early years practitioner?

Some of the confusion about how best to support the learning of young children seems to arise from an image of school learning and the behaviour of school teachers. The Foundation Stage guidance uses the term 'practitioner' to refer to all adults involved in supporting children's learning, but the words 'teach' and 'teaching' are used to describe those adults' behaviour. These words carry a weight of meaning that have created some difficulties in practice.

Some early years practitioners, and parents as well, appear to have linked early education and discussion about educational goals with their childhood memories of school, school work and teachers. These memories are often from a time later in childhood than the Foundation Stage, even if they are accurate memories.

Uneasy early years practitioners, especially without specific guidance from managers, have concluded that to support early learning they must behave close to their selective memories of what a 'teacher' does. This model has included greater adult direction of children's activities, including excessive use of paper and pencil activities through worksheets, a focus on group rather than individual work and more of a classroom feel, even for very young children. Anxiety about inspection and demands for evidence, based sometimes on direct experience of the behaviour of some inspectors, has increased the move to directive planning and interruption of children's actual learning for presumed learning.

Yet, of course, good nursery teachers do not behave at all the same way as teachers of primary school age children. Effective early years practitioners of a non-teaching background need to step away from the 'school teacher' model that is in their head. Good nursery teachers have long followed the threads of children's current thinking and created a welcoming environment that enables children to learn through play and nursery routines.

Janet Moyles, Sian Adams and Alison Musgrove have been involved in the SPEEL project (Study of Pedagogical Effectiveness in Early Learning). The view of the project is that teaching in the early years is more complex than in the rest of the educational system. Genuinely helpful adults need to follow the child's learning rather than a plan of activities that assume learning has taken place, so long the activity has been completed. The team acknowledge that allowing the child to drive the learning can seem or feel as if the practitioner is doing very little.

In the SPEEL project, practitioners were asked to produce a video showing what they believed to be effective adult behaviour to support the children's learning within their own practice. Few early years practitioners chose play situations. Far more often, they selected literacy and numeracy sessions, where they felt they were behaving like a teacher. The project highlighted how much early years practitioners need to feel valued and supported to provide developmentally appropriate activities for young children.

Being a helpful adult

Constructive feedback from adults can help children to focus on what has gone well, not just what has gone wrong. Friendly communication helps children to learn. All children will struggle over some skill or level of understanding and need adult guidance. They are far more likely to welcome suggestions and helpful hints from adults who are generally supportive rather than critical, and who are courteous with children even over something that has gone awry or wrong. Some children need especially to be supported in accepting compliments and recognising their achievements.

- Young children need to see themselves as learners, that they have learned in the past. Your familiarity with individual children can enable you, along with their parents, to remind the children of specific examples of what they have learned in the past.

- Enable children genuinely to learn from their mistakes. It is not enough to say, 'We all learn from our mistakes'. Adult behaviour has to stop the words from being an empty cliché. Children need to feel that 'good mistakes' and 'useful mistakes' help them to move on, because adults can spot what is confusing or only partly understood by young children.

- Be generous with help. Use your behaviour, words and body language to help children feel confident that it is fine to ask for help, for repeats of instructions, to say, 'I'm confused' or 'I don't understand'.

- Give generous time for children to practise, revisit activities and skills and to circle back in order to do it again. Children cannot learn well if they are moved on regularly because adults think there should be a certain range of activities or the morning must look different from the afternoon.

- Adult words and behaviour can support young children as they understand the process of learning. Skills can take time to learn; everyone needs to practise and the doing through practice can be enjoyable in itself. Young children need to discover the sheer pleasure to be felt in getting better at a skill, any skill, and then the delight in doing it again because now the climbing, the jigsaw, the story telling is so easy!

- Break down a skill or idea into smaller steps. Go back with a child or small group to the point at which they are competent or can understand. Then work on with them from that point of confidence to tackle what is confusing, difficult or even perhaps, you realise, too hard for now. Take your time and give children your friendly attention.

- You need to acknowledge children's difficulties and current frustrations. It is unhelpful to pretend everything is fine when it clearly is not for this child. When children are struggling, they are perplexed by adults who appear not to notice their difficulties.

- Useful and courteous phrases can be, 'You don't understand this at the moment' or 'You can't do this yet....' Children can then hear in your voice the sense that things can change; not knowing or struggling need not go on and on.

- Acknowledgement and an offer of help can be made with, 'I can see that you're finding this tough. Shall we see how I can help?' or 'That was a handy mistake you made, because now I understand where you get stuck. Can I show you....?'

- Be generous with time to appreciate, acknowledge and admire. Adults need to celebrate successes with children, often with friendly words and the respect of attention by looking and listening with genuine interest. Celebration does not always have to be lengthy or involve symbols like stickers.

- You support children's continued learning when you help them to register what they have managed before moving onto something else that is new and perhaps difficult. Give the time to notice and avoid being in a rush always to move on to the next activity or item on the plan.

- Acknowledgement can be words and body language that communicate a message like, 'You can manage this very well. You know, I think you're ready for....'

Personal, Social and Emotional Development

Three-year-olds are young children and it is important to emphasise this fact. Young children can be daunted and disheartened if too much is expected of them and adults do not tune into the three-year-old outlook. On the other hand, with supportive adults and a friendly, accessible environment for learning, three-year-olds can be very competent doers, impressive communicators and excellent company.

Adult anxiety about pushing children on in their development creates the twin disadvantages of expecting too much of three-year-olds and failing to notice and acknowledge how much they can do already. Three-year-olds' perspective on life, supported by their individual comments and questions, can be a delightfully fresh look at the world that reminds us as adults what it was like to approach experiences for the first time.

An increasing proportion of nursery schools, early years centres and pre-schools have children between two and a half years and three years, often because the settings have lost their four-year-olds to school. These very young children can be even more vulnerable when settings scarcely differentiate between threes and rising fives. You will find some examples in this book of two-year-olds and rising threes to help ground a strong developmental perspective.

Three-year-olds operate as individuals

Rising threes and three-year-olds undoubtedly have some social skills and they make friends (see page 14), but developmentally this age group approaches the world from a very individual perspective.

These young children learn by building on their own perspective and moving outwards to the viewpoint and lives of other people. Their social world is grounded in what they know already and what makes sense to them from personal experience so far.

Young children are sometimes described as egocentric. This term is acceptable, so long as it is not weighted with the negative overtones of self-centred or selfish. Three-year-olds are focused on themselves and their own perspective. You will see this individual orientation in their learning, their questions and when they are puzzled about skills or ideas. Rising threes and three-year-olds are centred on themselves in a positive way but, in a supportive environment, they are capable of prosocial behaviour. The extent to which they can focus on other people (see the examples on pages 14-16) has to be admired against the developmental backdrop of this personal orientation.

Do three-year-olds do groups?

Three-year-olds need personal attention and the sense that they have an active part to play in what is happening right now. The more they feel disconnected from an activity or event, the harder it is for them to focus and so to learn. Three-year-olds, especially once they are accustomed to nursery or playgroup routines, can usually manage short gathering times in a group. But young children need to see the point in what is happening. Three-year-olds find it hard to tolerate large groups because there is too much waiting and not enough personal attention. Even a year later, many four-year-olds will struggle within large groups with activities that are, from their point of view, boring.

Many three-year-olds relish a good conversation and will start one themselves (see the examples on pages 25-26), but they have difficulty with large group communication, including circle time, especially if the practitioner is insensitive to their level of development. Rising threes and three-year-olds also find it hard to wait in order to voice what they want to say. From the three-year-old perspective, something interesting enough to share with adults or other children needs to be said right now or at the least very soon.

For example

Rising threes and three-year-olds are more able to manage some small group time when they can be active or they have a practical focus.

■ Three-year-olds who are familiar with the routine can enjoy short singing times, with plenty of accompanying hand movements. There is a good example in the video *The High/Scope Approach to Under Threes*. A small group of two-year-olds and rising threes has an enthusiastic singing session with a rousing version of 'The wheels on the bus'. The children are not required to sit in a neat circle or even to sit down at all. Some children are sitting on an adult lap, one or two are standing up, all the better to get an effective whirling arm movement. At one point, two children are draped over the back and shoulders of the male practitioner in the group. The children are enthused, active, appropriately noisy and clearly having an excellent time.

■ A mixed group of three- and four-year-olds that I observed in New River Green was quite restless after lunch. The practitioner had accepted some books that a couple of children wanted to be read as stories to the group, but had the good sense to observe the shifting bottoms and arms and suggested some action songs instead. There was no criticism of the children, simply a descriptive comment, 'I think we're all too restless for a story. We'll have some songs'. (See page 27 for a further description of this example.)

■ In Poplar Play I watched a mixed group of children, aged from rising twos to seven-year-olds (the holiday playscheme children), sit peaceably on a blanket spread out on the grass. They were busy eating their toast for a late breakfast snack. The atmosphere was relaxed and children were enjoying having a chat, with each other and with the adults.

■ Social mealtimes are more feasible as group together time for three-year-olds. They have a practical focus and there is a friendly atmosphere. (See also the example on page 20.)

(See page 60 for details of people and places mentioned in examples.)

Enthusiastic learners

Rising threes and three-year-olds will have learned at home with their families, during their time with childminders and in early years settings that offer childcare for children as young as babies. Three-year-olds will continue to learn within their family and this aspect of their young lives is one reason for the importance of

Food for thought

Three-year-olds find it difficult to cope with long sit-down group sessions when they cannot relate to the content of the group activity.

Some early years settings felt, and some still appear to feel, that three-year-olds should be involved in half-hour, or even hour long, mat sessions to promote early literacy in a formal way with sounds and letters. The three-year-olds (and many four-year-olds too!) find this activity hard to tolerate because it is boring.

Young children's restlessness, and desire to sneak off somewhere much more interesting, is then sometimes interpreted as disruptive behaviour. When adults feel under pressure - shown by comments like 'We have to do this', 'It's a national requirement' and 'They have to learn to concentrate' - it is easier to blame the children than challenge deeply inappropriate expectations and methods.

Wise practitioners have decided that there is something awry with the activity, not with the children, and have returned to far more developmentally appropriate ways to support early literacy.

Marjorie Ouvry tells an engaging version of this dilemma in her presentations about outdoor play and the importance of being able to move. She observed a formal mat session from which one three-year-old boy removed himself and strode towards the outdoor area with the heartfelt comment of, 'I'm far too young for this!'

Food for thought

Unreflective discussion about early education implies that children do not really start to learn unless and until they have joined an early educational setting. But, of course children have started to learn before they enter what is called the Foundation Stage in England. Early learning is not the same as early education.

Being a helpful adult

Your own setting will seem familiar to you but you will help three-year-olds, and their parents and carers, by looking at the environment and routines with a fresh eye.

- What is the group experience like for a three-year-old? What might be similar to home and what will be different?

- What do group routines require of three-year-olds and how can they be enabled to cope and feel competent?

- Adult feelings are involved as well and parents can have to cope with their own sadness at separation, as well as the leap of trust needed to leave their young children with people who are initially strangers.

- Are your expectations of three-year-olds realistic? What about your expectations of parents? In what ways do you help children and adults to feel secure?

- Some three-year-olds cannot wait to get into nursery - perhaps they are already familiar from dropping off an older sibling - and wave a cheery farewell. Some parents who have done an excellent job of preparing their son or daughter for nursery or playgroup may have overlooked their own feelings and welcome some support themselves. For many parents it is the first time they do not know how their child has spent their day.

partnership with parents. Children who have been cared for within the family up to now will experience their first out-of-home setting as they enter a nursery, pre-school or playgroup at the beginning of the Foundation Stage. Other children will simply continue with their childminder or early years nursery or centre. Three-year-olds are naturally curious. Unless their enthusiasm has been stunted by harsh treatment or excessively passive activities, they are keen to learn and explore. Young children do not have to be persuaded to learn; it is much more the case that adults need to be careful that they do not inadvertently block young learning. Attentive observation of three-year-olds supports what is highlighted by the research into brain development. Rising threes and three-year-olds learn by making direct connections between new experiences or ideas and what they already know and understand. If they are required to make too big a leap between the old and new, then three-year-olds are perplexed and, if put under pressure to manage something that is too hard, then they are unhappy.

Three-year-olds benefit from a combination of familiar and new. They may like to try new activities but some children will very much want the familiar. Repetition and slight variations on familiar themes support learning. Three-year-olds (and fours and fives as well) learn best by having choice and control over their learning. They need time to explore and their extension of knowledge and skills is best driven by their interests today. Three-year-olds are keen to push out the boundaries of ability on materials they want to handle now and the topic of conversation that enthuses them this moment.

Feeling secure, feeling that 'I belong'

The practical lessons of observational research on young children in day care are that they need to be enabled to form close and affectionate relationships with their non-family carers. Rising threes and three-year-olds need to feel that they are noticed, liked and have become a valued part of the social network that is a nursery, playgroup or a childminder's home. The research into day care highlights that supporting children's personal, social and emotional development is utterly central

to their well-being; it is never some optional extra to get around to once you have covered the 'more important' areas of development.

Some three-year-olds will be coping with separation from their parent(s) at this stage of their early experience. However, the separation experience will be different for individual children. Separating from the main carer will be a significant issue, when this setting is the first out-of-home care for a child. But some three-year-olds simply continue in their nursery or centre or with their childminder, the settling and separation will have been managed earlier.

Barbara Tizard, and her team at Thomas Coram Research Unit during the 1980s and 90s, confirmed how much positive outcomes for young children depend on their forming close personal relationships in out-of-home care. Barbara Tizard identified three key characteristics of supportive relationships for young children: familiarity, attachment and responsiveness. Young children need to become familiar with an out-of-home setting. They need to form a close attachment to one or two early years practitioners. They need those adults to show a high level of responsiveness to them as individuals.

These findings are as relevant now as they ever were; children have not changed. One of the blocks to the application of such findings remains the divide in the UK between what is called 'child care' and what is called 'early education'. The latter will not work to children's benefit without a strong caring orientation and that means recognition that children need to feel that adults respond to them as individuals.

Do three-year-olds have a sense of community?

Young children view the world from their personal perspective outwards into what they recognise as the broader social network for themselves and their family. Three-year-olds need a sense of themselves, of personal identity and a secure sense of self-worth, before they can make much sense at all of the sources of identity of others.

Three-year-olds are focused on their own direct experience: they assume that their own family and neighbourhood are the blueprint for everyone's life, until they discover to the contrary. Young children also notice and may comment upon differences in dress or language that reflect different cultures and faiths locally. They start by finding differences of interest, or not, but they do not automatically believe that different is wrong or less acceptable.

Children are not born prejudiced or bigoted, but they are enthusiastic learners and imitators of the behaviour of familiar and loved adults. Adult divisions can then be reflected in children's words and choice of play companions, on ethnic group lines or religious, sectarian lines as in Northern Ireland. Parents and early years practitioners may underestimate the extent to which even three-year-olds hear and imitate negative attitudes rife in their local neighbourhood (see the research about children in Northern Ireland in *What Does it Mean to be Five?*, page 44). Early years practitioners support children by giving serious consideration to the diversity in the neighbourhood, as well as recognising tensions. Offensive comments or rejecting behaviour need to be handled when they arise. A firm yet courteous approach will help children at least to recognise alternative ways of behaving.

Being a helpful adult

This section is not saying that practitioners should avoid conversation or activities related to less familiar cultures. Helpful adults need to look for the likely connections of understanding.

- Support for the development of positive attitudes has to build out from familiar experience. It is unrealistic to aim to promote three-year-olds' understanding of a wide range of unfamiliar cultures or faiths, that they cannot experience in daily life in a way that makes sense to them. Three-year-olds are in the process of understanding the familiar social and cultural groupings to which they, their families and their friends belong.

- There is little point in involving three-year-olds (or fours for that matter) in a flurry of multicultural activities that scarcely connect to their current experience. Young children cannot relate to a long list of celebrations or cultural traditions; they simply get confused.

- Look at what currently interests the children and build a little from that base. The connections might be to food or music, to family celebrations like welcoming a new baby, or to places and traditions that connect with the families whose children attend your setting.

For example

The case studies in the Save the Children consultation pack (see Further reading and resources, page 57) demonstrate how active involvement of young children will engage them and promote learning.

■ Hillside Nursery in Hackney, London involved rising threes and three-year-olds in the plans for a visit to a farm. The children were working within a long-term project about farms and farm animals. These young children were part of a round table discussion about what they would do on their visit. They used smiley and grumpy faces on sticks to vote for and against each proposal. The children also had writing materials and some chose to make their own 'notes' of the meeting. The children then worked with the practitioners on what should be written into the letter arranging their visit. During the visit the children made drawings and plans and back at the nursery made a papier maché model of the farm. Through the planning, the actual visit and the creative work that followed, the practitioners were careful to follow the children's interests and wishes.

Of course, in any discussion or consultation adults often need to offer some options. Young children, depending on their age and experience to date, may find it hard to envisage possibilities. But adults can add some useful information without imposing their own goals and structure. You will find similar examples in *What Does it Mean to be Four?* on pages 14 and 16.

The importance of making friends

Friendships matter to young children and consultation exercises with three- and four-year-olds have often highlighted through children's spontaneous remarks that being with their friends is a major source of pleasure in nurseries and playgroups.

Rising threes and three-year-olds make friends when their social environment enables them to get to know other children well. Three-year-olds can be adept at temporary social alliances in drop-in settings but genuine friendship can only develop when children meet others on a regular basis, not necessarily every day. Early years practitioners are often aware of the importance of continuity of adults in creating an emotionally secure environment. However, from the children's point of view it can be important that there is some constancy in the group of children. Otherwise three-year-olds can effectively face a continual 'cocktail party' scenario.

For example

In order for children to make friends, they need regular contact as well as an environment in which it is easy to develop shared games and keep enjoyable company. Rising threes and three-year-olds can cope with a predictable pattern that they check with their parent or carer:

■ At nearly three years of age, my daughter Tanith knew that Wednesday was the day she visited a drop-in at the small, local community nursery, accompanied by me or her nanny. Tanith had met and got on well with Matthew, who also attended regularly. They both looked forward to meeting once a week in this predictable way.

■ Three-year-old Marie was with a childminder each day and was the only child who attended every day of the week. However, as Marie's mother described to me, her daughter was completely clear about the pattern of attendance of the other children. Marie liked to check on what day it was each morning, then she had clear recall of which child(ren) she would see and play with. Marie was confident about what would happen each day and did not find it upsetting that she was the only daily child, because this pattern was normal for her.

■ In contrast, I have spoken with teams from several pre-schools and playgroups who have variable attendance patterns that suit parents. Young children cannot build enough predictable social contact within the setting in order to make friends with other, individual children. The whole group can be up to 20-25 and the faces vary from day to day.

Three-year-olds do not only make close social contact with their age peers. They need their peers for some forms of play, but young children also like contact with younger and older children. In early years settings catering for a wide age range, from babies to four-year-olds, there are social gains for all the children in having some mixed age times.

- Contact between the ages is part of normal family life and of links between local families. Group settings can and should enable contact across the age range.
- Even three-year-olds can be adept at the repetitive games that babies and toddlers adore and at making them chortle. The older children also often like to 'read' to toddlers by telling the story to the pages and illustrations of a familiar book.
- The slightly older children begin to adjust their style of communication. They show an understanding, an empathy, that babies and toddlers need simpler words and more body language.

Learning social skills as a three-year-old

Young children can learn useful social skills through early childhood, but such skills do not automatically appear with the passing of birthdays. Children steadily learn how to play with and communicate with other children. They also learn the different patterns and routines that work between homes, family or childminder's, and a group setting, even one with a positive home-like feel.

Three-year-olds are also learning the social skills of what to do, and what to expect for yourself, when social communication goes awry. Adults are sometimes insistent that children say sorry. Yet an inflexible approach is more likely to convince children that this particular 'magic word' stops adults nagging you. Three-year-olds often cannot predict the consequences of their actions and sometimes there has been a genuine accident. Given time and choices, three-year-olds can use different ways to say and show 'sorry' and learn a bit more about the feelings of the child, or adult, who has been bumped, overlooked or whose feelings were hurt (the toughest one for a three-year-old to grasp.)

Being a helpful adult

- Adults need to respect three-year-olds' friendships, rather than telling them that such and such a child is their friend. Watch and listen, then children's behaviour will enable you to learn about their social network.
- You need to organise a day and the environment so that children can make choices easily about with whom they will play, who will sit with them at the table, even when and with whom they will have their drink and snack.
- The more adults drive a session or day by what they want to happen, the less children have any genuine hope of socialising and learning three-year-old social skills. Children cannot make friends if adults keep organising them into groups or telling the children to move onto another activity.
- You can help children to develop social skills, when you take the time to observe what individual children find difficult as well as easy, rather than classifying social struggles swiftly as a behavioural problem. Set a good example yourself in friendliness, showing social skills in action.
- Be generous with your time and attention. Three-year-olds who have to compete for adult attention or affection have limited emotional energy to make social contact.

Rising threes and three-year-olds are in the process of tackling the practicalities of social skills. Adults help by recognising when support is needed and offering it in a practical way.

- Three-year-olds make contact in a personal way. When very young children enter a group setting, a busy room can look overwhelming to them. Large open rooms, such as many playgroups and pre-schools use, can be daunting. Three-year-olds can experience the kind of emotional overload that adults feel when they enter a lively party and don't know anybody.

- Young children see activities in progress and think that everyone seems already to have a friend. Three-year-olds are a varied group of individuals, so some boys and girls may plunge into a recognisable activity, others will hover, uncertain what to do, and some will be visibly distressed, only reassured by the continued presence of a parent or familiar carer.

Three-year-olds find it hard to step back from their own perspective, especially if emotions are highly charged. Adult communication needs to be simpler and the skills of problem-solving and conflict resolution are at their most basic. Four-year-olds can manage more of the communication skills and mental stepping back (see page 15 in *What Does it Mean to be Four?*).

For example

In New River Green I was at the dough table with four children, a mixed group of three- and four-year-olds. I did not know any of the children's names and referred to one boy without being able to use his name. I asked Jake (three years old), 'Have you got some play dough for him?'

Jake showed good three-year-old skills and told me the boy's name. It was an unusual name to me and I got it wrong when I repeated it back to Jake. He was patient and repeated the name twice so I could say it correctly. Later in the same day, at another activity, Jake spontaneously told me the names of some other children. The likely explanation seemed to be that Jake wanted me to be able to address other children personally and properly.

First and foremost, three-year-olds need you to understand the skills they have to tackle and to support them from the level of skill they have at the moment. Children are learning:

- How to approach children who are already involved in an activity they would like to join. How do you move in without annoying the group or being rejected? Sometimes no strategy will work, because the group is closed.
- How to invite other children to join their own activity, so that this child can create some companionship.
- How to leave a group when this child has had enough and how to extract themselves from a child who wants to play with them when they do not, at the moment, feel the same way.
- Three-year-olds, and older children, often find it hard to establish a comfortable balance of followers and leaders, and to realise that some ways of being active in a group make other children see you as bossy.

Three-year-olds and prosocial behaviour

Three-year-olds are capable of showing prosocial behaviour: an awareness of the feelings of others and sometimes acting with the interests of somebody else to the forefront. Research on the development of prosocial behaviour highlights that young children can be considerate of others, show kindness and manage sometimes the behaviour that adults call 'sharing', 'turn taking' and 'thinking about other people'. However, three-year-olds need to feel emotionally secure themselves. Children who feel liked and are confident they can easily get attention from familiar carers are able to be generous in their turn. In contrast, three-year-olds who have to compete with their peers for adult time and affection, do not learn to be considerate of other children, who they have identified accurately as their rivals for adult time.

Three-year-olds do not learn to be considerate or kind in one big developmental step, nor do they show this kind of behaviour every minute of every day. Adults need to hold realistic expectations for children, with the backdrop of 'Would you expect an adult to behave in this way?' taking a meaningful parallel for what you are asking of three-year-olds. Three-year-olds who feel secure are happy sometimes to help another child, take turns even on a much valued piece of equipment and to offer comfort in times of distress. They will probably not be able to explain why these actions are the 'right' way to behave other than that it is 'much nicer if we are friendly to each other' or the reciprocal feel of 'I help her and she helps me'. It really does not matter if three-year-olds cannot yet put into words why we behave in this way.

Feelings and three-year-olds

Rising threes and three-year-olds experience the full range of feelings but they are still coming to terms with how to express those emotions through actions and words. They also have much to learn about other people's feelings, both children and adults.

Children can develop emotional literacy throughout the early years but this is a steady development and three-year-olds have some way to go. Emotional literacy means the ability to recognise and understand our own emotions and those of others. Over the early years children who are emotionally supported by caring adults can become more able to:

- Recognise that they have feelings
- Link words to those feelings and talk about them in an 'I feel ...' way
- Recognise that other people, children and adults, have feelings too, some of which are similar to their own
- Recognise some ways in which strong feelings arise, experienced by themselves or others
- Learn, with support, ways to express feelings in ways that do not hurt others, physically or emotionally.

Rising threes and three-year-olds may be confused about their feelings and will not always have the words to explain. Much also depends on how far the familiar adults in their lives have used communication to explain and show about emotions. This age group can respond swiftly and move at speed from happiness and excitement to distress or frustration, but also with support, back again to being happy. They find it

Food for thought

Children are learning from all aspects of their experience, not just in the ways and from the activities that adults judge are 'learning times'. Three-year-olds will, of course, bring their previous experience into your setting, group or your home as a childminder. Sometimes there may be a period when they learn your ways and observe the good example you set.

If three-year-olds have settled and are familiar with a new setting, then further struggles with prosocial behaviour may be explained by the reality that sharing or consideration for others is not made easy here. In some settings the adults have not properly thought through what they mean and require by sharing or realised that the routines may make turn taking hard for three-year-olds.

Young children also learn through observation. They are not guided towards prosocial behaviour by nagging adults who say they 'ought to share' or 'must be kind', especially if the example set by those same adults is neither kind nor models behaviour that demonstrates sharing.

hard to re-direct themselves once the strong feelings have welled and very strong feelings sometimes frighten them. They need to feel emotionally safe in order to calm down and such support often needs to be physical: the comfort of touch and cuddle and sometimes the safety of arms that communicate, 'I'm not going to let you hurt yourself or anyone else'.

Three-year-olds use body language and words to express their feelings, and may well have begun to use familiar characters to do the talking for them: teddy, a puppet or other favourite cuddly toys or a liked character in a familiar story. Their feelings are sometimes expressed deliberately in this way through a play channel.

The feelings expressed, or suppressed, by three years will already reflect their experience from home and out-of-home care. Threes and rising fours have observed and learned some lessons about adult emotional literacy, or the lack of it. They may have learned that familiar adults do not take some of their feelings seriously or do not want to observe certain emotions. Children may be told, 'There's nothing to be frightened about; it's only a worm' or 'Take that angry look off your face!' Children learn about feelings that are acceptable to adults and those which are better hidden. Perhaps you are not supposed to get over excited or 'big boys don't cry'.

Learning about right and wrong

Over the early years of childhood, children progress in moral development. Helpful adults need to recognise the different strands to what children are learning as well as being sensible and realistic about what children of different ages are likely to understand. Children are learning about moral behaviour, understanding and judgement.

Young children learn about what familiar adults regard as acceptable and unacceptable ways of behaving. So long as adults are consistent, rising threes and three-year-olds can have a fairly clear idea of what their familiar adults want in terms of children's behaviour. Three-year-olds can have worked out what makes those adults pleased, sad, irritated and seriously annoyed. They are still working to the theory that all life works the same way as their own home life or familiar carers outside their family. They can be perplexed, and sometimes distressed, when behaviour they have learned to be acceptable elsewhere does not meet with friendly approval in this new setting or is actually judged to be unacceptable. For instance, settings vary a great deal in how much they encourage children to access materials and organise themselves.

Three-year-olds in a happy atmosphere often want to please adults but they as yet have only a hazy idea of the underlying principles and reasons. They need simple explanations linked to experiences that make sense to them. Abstract ideas of 'right' and 'wrong' are too unconnected for three-year-olds, but they can take on board simple ground rules that make sense in their setting. Three-year-olds struggle with the abstract moral philosophy, but they are keen observers of interaction and communication. If adults fail to set a good example about the behaviour they want, then children are likely to follow what the adults do rather than what they say should be done.

Three-year-old concentration

Three-year-olds have developed skills of attention, of looking and listening. Given an activity of interest to them and no interruptions, many can concentrate well and are increasingly able to get themselves back to the activity if the diversion is mild or of their own choosing. There are many examples in this book of three-year-olds concentrating well and for periods of time - see pages 11, 20 or 33.

Three-year-olds find it difficult to concentrate when they are required to keep still or sit down. They can concentrate while on the move, for instance in absorbing outdoor activity. Often the visible option of movement is enough. I have learned from several nurseries that taking some of the indoor activities outside has increased usage by the more active children. It seems that simply having the freedom to leave means that children do not feel they have to move away. They continue to have a choice.

Sharing in their own care and routines

Three-year-olds are on the road towards independence, but it is a steady process. In an emotionally secure environment, young children can show and practise skills of self-reliance within daily routines and they are already able to share in much of their own care. Three-year-olds can usually:

- Manage much of their own toileting and simple hygiene like hand washing.

- Feed themselves and handle drinks, although not all the time and there will be some spillage.

- Be involved and competent in getting ready for meals, handing round food and tidying up afterwards. They are able to make choices about food and drink.
- Dress and undress, with help for the trickier fastenings - shoelaces are difficult for some time yet. They express preferences about what they will wear.

Three-year-olds are able to be an active member of a family home or group setting, so long as adults allow and enable this behaviour. Three-year-olds can be adept at making choices, planning ahead for the day and commenting on how the day or session has gone, tidying up, helping in food preparation and simple administration tasks such as running messages or returning the register to the office in a group.

The layout of settings and the behaviour of adults can make a big difference to three-year-olds' concentration.

Three-year-olds can be distracted by the layout in a setting where there are no peaceful corners. Children who could concentrate on building will give up if their constructions are regularly knocked over.

Children need enough materials. Concentration is disrupted in a nursery or family home where adults promote the kind of sharing that actually means 'hand it over now'.

When adults have narrow views about concentration, they sometimes insist on activities, such as completing worksheets that break into the child's current absorption. It is not necessarily a positive sign that children are willing to complete an activity when they show little enthusiasm for the task.

Young children's concentration can be badly disrupted by over-planning that requires children to move on from one activity to another, perhaps from table to table at a time call from adults. This pattern has been justified to me on the grounds that children must experience a full curriculum. But adults' actions actually disrupt attention and the flow of learning over the days.

Rigid routines about dismantling and tidying up can disrupt attention as well as children's view that their work is valued. There are some realistic difficulties with shared premises, such as church halls. However, some settings that do not experience these pressures nevertheless get into unwise habits. Apart from having safe places to keep an unfinished project, adults and children can use cameras to record work in progress or take a permanent record of something that took a lot of time and which really does have to be taken apart now.

Food for thought
There is great variety in the level of confidence in this age group but much of the variation is also created by adult behaviour.

- Can three-year-olds access play materials to make a choice or are they presented with activities or told what is on offer?

- Children cannot exercise choice unless materials are organised in ways that three-year-olds can find and select, as well as tidy away when they have finished. The workshop or learning space way of organising enables children to access materials that are stored around the setting in containers that they can manage.

- Are the children given an active part to play in routines or do they have to wait, perhaps with a rather unwieldy group activity, while other adults tidy up or lay tables?

- Do the adults value what young children can learn and practise from relaxed self-reliance and involvement in routines? Or are such activities downgraded as 'care' in contrast to the more valued 'education'?

- A very restricted 'learning through play' approach can also be disruptive of children's potential to learn through involvement in daily routines. Of course, children often recycle their experience through play, but the learning does not have to pass into play to become valuable or real.

For example

Active and social mealtimes are perfectly possible with three-year-olds and even younger children. The key is that adults value these times of the day, give them time to unfold and support children's efforts. I spent an enjoyable lunchtime with a group of young children aged 18 months to three years in Saplings Nursery. The whole atmosphere was one of a relaxed, shared meal that was valued as a social occasion. The oldest children were rising threes, yet they were all competent and showed awareness of the needs of their peers and quiet pleasure in helping out. The practitioner sitting at the table with the children was relaxed and offered help if necessary. But mainly he was a calm presence at the lunch table, eating his lunch with the children and helping to make it a social and involved mealtime.

- These young children helped to dish up for themselves and for each other. One two-year-old held a large yoghurt carton with both hands as another child spooned out what she wanted to add to her mashed apple.

- The children poured their own drinks, although adult help was always available if wanted.

- There were remarkably few spills. The once or twice that it happened, children either fetched the dishcloth themselves or the practitioner reminded, 'It's the yellow one, hanging up over there'. Children were then encouraged to hang the cloth back up again.

- Conversations started, paused as someone ate and then resumed. Between the main course and dessert one girl decided to move across to the other table. The practitioner simply acknowledged the move with, 'Oh, do you want to sit with your friend?'

(A longer version of this example first appeared in *Helping Babies and Toddlers Learn; a Guide to Good Practice with Under Threes* by Jennie Lindon published by National Early Years Network.)

For example

In New River Green I sat with Rosie (three years) in an area with a table and pull-out drawers with jigsaws as well as other materials.

- Rosie started to chat, telling me what she planned to do: 'I'm going to do drawing. (pause) I'm going to do the puzzle, then drawing and then I'm going to go outside'.

- She was able to pull out the drawer and choose a wooden jigsaw. We tipped it out onto the table. Rosie used her finger to hop from piece to piece and she sang a tuneful ditty that was mainly the words 'Froggy, froggy, froggy'.

- Rosie told me, 'I can't do this puzzle', but it soon became clear that she knew how to sort out the pieces and fit them together. I said, 'You were teasing me. You can do this puzzle.' Rosie giggled in reply.

- In between completing the puzzle with confidence, Rosie commented and showed me other items of interest close by. She focused back onto the puzzle each time with no difficulty. It may have helped that we were in a quiet corner of the centre, with only Rosie and myself at this table.

Involvement in self-care and the daily routines matters a great deal for three-year-olds (and fours and fives just as much). Children learn much through play, but they do not learn only through play. They learn and apply many ideas through involvement in what makes the day roll along, in a group setting or home with a childminder.

The skills of self-reliance and self-care are very important to children and can be overlooked when adults develop tunnel vision about some aspects of development, usually the intellectual side:

- Rising threes and three-year-olds can be able and enthusiastic helpers in an early years setting or family home, their own or that of a childminder. Three-year-olds and their slightly older companions develop their self-confidence and emotional well-being by feeling like active members of the setting, rather than children who watch and wait.

Help yourself to water

Food for thought
- There is very good reason for early years practitioners to view the whole early years curriculum through children's personal, social and emotional development, along with their skills of communication in a social context.
- The continued learning of three-year-olds will unfold reliably from that priority. You can fairly evaluate any plans and activities from that perspective, both the forward planning and the review of how a day or week has gone from the children's point of view.

- Involvement in daily routines supports emotional and social development, especially when adults model both the giving and accepting of help. Children's sense of identity is supported when they feel part of their home or group setting and the experience creates firm foundations for self-esteem.

- When adults show that they value children's growing self-reliance, rising threes and three-year-olds are directly supported in a positive disposition to learn (see also page 6). The children have direct experience that they can learn and they can see the results.

- Practice in self-care and involvement in ordinary daily routines are an excellent vehicle for children's intellectual development. These are practical experiences that make direct sense to three-year-olds as they use skills of recall, understanding sequence (in dressing or daily routines with 'First we, then we...') and simple cause and effect ('We have to remember to... or else...'). Thinking skills are used as children weigh up options, make choices and do simple negotiation when not everyone wants to do the same.

- Daily routines over mealtimes are ideal for practical early maths, using counting, and matching people to their crockery and utensils. There is considerably less confusion over abstract ideas because the connection is swiftly made to a hands-on application.

Communication, Language and Literacy

Three-year-olds can be effective communicators, using their own spoken language as well as sensitivity to the non-verbal messages from the body language of familiar adults and children. Relaxed communication should be an integral part of the day with three-year-olds, with adults setting a good example of listening and looking, with sharing the lead-in conversations.

The skills of communication

Rising threes and three-year-olds are a varied group, depending on their temperament as well as their experiences to date. Some are far more chatty, articulate and questioning than their fellow three-year-olds. By now most children have an impressive vocabulary and it is a challenging task to note down all their words and the ways in which they use them. Three-year-olds who experience a relaxed and communicative atmosphere will continue to add new words, as well as combine their words in phrases that show their ability to use language for different purposes.

For example

One way to heighten our awareness of children's language and their ideas is to be alert to the questions that children ask spontaneously. This is a useful shift away from the tendency for adults to focus on the questions they want to ask the children (see also page 26). What interests three-year-olds enough to phrase a question?

By nearly two and a half years of age, my daughter Tanith had definitely grasped that she was a girl and her brother was a boy. Over the next few months she returned through questions to individuals in our family and local network of friends - who was a boy or a girl? Her questions often seemed to me to come out of the blue, but of course she must have been thinking about this interesting issue and the questions emerged when she wanted to ask and have an answer.

At just three years old, Drew was with me in a part of the local neighbourhood where there were high tower blocks. He was used to looking at three storeys in our immediate locality. With some concern, he indicated the high tower block and asked, 'Will it fall down?' I reassured him that, 'No, the towers are built so they are strong'. Drew still looked slightly dubious and said, 'My Lego towers fall down'.

I was walking locally and passed a young boy, who looked about three years old, strolling with his dad who was pushing a baby in the buggy. The boy appeared to be in the middle of a conversation important to him and was asking, 'You and me, Dad - we're not girls, are we?'

At lunch time in New River Green, James (three years) was interested in the salt that the early years practitioner added to her own lunch. She explained, 'When you are a grown-up, you decide if you want extra salt on your food.'

Three-year-olds do not simply have a large vocabulary; they know and use different types of words. Helpful adults need to tune into what children say and are interested to say at the moment. Three-year-old learning progresses from this individual point.

- Toddlers' first set of words will be the names of familiar people and objects that they see and handle in daily life. In terms of grammar, these words are the nouns.

- If language development is progressing without difficulties, then by eighteen months to about two years of age, young children are also using a range of words that apply to actions (the verbs). These words refer to what people are doing or what the child wants to have happen.

- Once a young child has naming and action words, then they have the conceptual and language base to use words that communicate very simple ideas. Two-year-olds show that they are ready to describe characteristics of the world around them, that mean something to a child. They use words that add to the naming words (adjectives) and the action words (adverbs).

- So the first descriptive or ideas words that young children use will relate closely to what they can experience directly through their senses. There is no point in adults deciding that they will promote the understanding of specific abstract ideas such as colour or shape, if the child has not yet homed in on what these ideas are like in hands-on experience. (See the examples on pages 25 and 31.)

- Three-year-olds are much clearer now about how objects relate together in ways that they can see and directly experience. So they are more likely to use words like 'in', 'on' or 'under' that describe simple connections between objects (grammatically, the prepositions).

Being a helpful adult

You can make a real difference when you make the effort to look through children's eyes and observe the world from their perspective.

- Recognise and recall that what is obvious to you is not yet obvious to children. This difference between your adult perspective and that of a three-year-old is especially crucial when you consider abstract concepts. You have lived with ideas like size, colour and the symbolism of number for many, many years. They seem so clear to you, of course they make sense. Not to three-year-olds, they don't!

- Adults need to use their mature thinking power to imagine and recall what it is like not to know an item of knowledge, a set of steps towards a goal, an idea, a connection between ideas, the answer to a question or how to do something.

- Three-year-olds who have had varied experiences have often developed their own interests that are reflected in a slightly more specialist vocabulary. The words used by some three-year-olds may well show their interest in diggers and other large-scale machines or transport, dinosaurs, fantasy creatures or different kinds of flowers or creatures. Three-year-olds use a wide variety of grammatical structures and they learn both the regular and irregular grammatical forms by listening to what is said in their hearing. English is an especially difficult language with exceptions to practically every grammatical rule, so it is usual that three-year-olds, and fours and fives, make mistakes by extending the basic rule to words that are exceptions, for instance, 'eated' rather than 'ate'.

- Of course, three-year-olds and their slightly older companions learn the grammatical forms that they hear from adults and children in their neighbourhood. Different versions of English, between social and cultural groups, often use variations in the basic grammar ('we was..' rather than 'we were..' or 'me' instead of 'I').

Three-year-olds also use their language to serve different ends in their play, conversation with children and adults and their involvement in daily routines.

- Three years use their language to narrate what they are doing (see the example on page 34) and direct their own play.

- Three-year-olds can use their language to tell and describe as part of a conversation. They can use words to share immediate interests but also to recall incidents in the past, as well as planning a little into the future.

- In simple versions, three-year-olds can explain, justify and sometimes argue their point of view. The fact that sometimes they may be arguing with you as the adult should not lead you to overlook the impressive use of language!

Talking and thinking

If you look at the Foundation Stage guidance you will notice that the separate strands recognise that children learn to use spoken language for self-direction and thinking as well as for communication.

- Young children like to talk about ideas or possibilities that make sense in their social world. Three-year-olds need to speak their thoughts and to voice an idea out loud very soon after thinking it. They find it tough to keep quiet if something has interested or intrigued them. They want to share, especially in a conversational home or setting.

- When three-year-olds say something out loud, it helps them to firm up their opinions or ideas. The words give the ideas a more definite form. Young children need to be active in their language in order to support their thinking.

- Three-year-olds (and fours and fives, too) use speaking out loud to themselves as a way to guide their actions and weigh up possibilities (see the examples on pages 20 or 34). They literally think out loud and continue to do so until five or six years of age. Adults who require children to be quiet will actually block their thinking and learning.

- If they find a group activity interesting, children will want to speak out and swiftly. Personal conversations or very small groups are crucial. Otherwise active and interested children who are listening closely can be labelled as disruptive and lacking in concentration, simply because they want to contribute now.

For example

It is important that adults follow the flow of what children want to talk about in conversation. Of course, sometimes you will start a topic. But, in settings or a family home with a friendly, conversational atmosphere, children do not have to be persuaded to talk.

In New River Green a practitioner had arrived at the table with a fresh batch of bright red playdough. She ladled out some of it on the table, explaining that the rest was for the toddlers. She also explained it was still hot. Rosie (three years) and Tyrone (four years) were very interested in the dough. Rosie wanted to know why the dough was hot and the practitioner explained that she had just cooked it fresh for everyone. Tyrone wanted to know how the practitioner cooked the dough. Both children were fascinated with the fact that the dough was not cool and they tentatively touched it. The dough was now warm rather than hot.

In the afternoon Rosie recalled the time we spent together in the morning (see the example on page 20). We came together in the garden and Rosie commented, 'You went away when I had my milk'. I replied, 'You were busy, so I went to another part of the nursery'. Rosie then continued, 'I didn't do another jigsaw because you'd gone'. I answered, 'I'm sorry I'd gone. But I did enjoy doing the jigsaw and looking at the fish with you.'

Being a helpful adult

Questions have a place in communication: from the child to you and from you to the children. But you do not want your use of questions to unbalance communication, nor for children to gain the impression that adults usually ask the questions and children give the answers.

- Closed questions are those to which there is really only one answer. There are times in a day when a closed question is appropriate, for instance, 'Has anybody seen where I put the register?' or 'Would you like another baked potato?'

- A useful balance from adults needs a range of open-ended questions and questioning requests. These are adult comments to which there are several possible answers, for instance, 'That's a very interesting fact about spiders. How did you find that out?' or 'Any ideas about how we can unravel all this string?'

- It is best to avoid the run of testing questions, to which you as an adult know the answer and you are asking only to find out if the child knows. Early years practitioners who feel they should show 'teacher-like' behaviour (see the comments on page 8) are sometimes tempted to use such questions to provide evidence of a child's learning or to extend an activity in ways that suit adult plans. Children feel under pressure when they are asked many testing questions about colour, shape, number and other ideas. They do not mind a few such requests, especially if the context is playful, like, 'Let's see if we can find...?' or 'Who's got sharp eyes here...?'

Winston and Jon in New River Green (both three years old) found and put on hard hats, one yellow and one red. Winston said, 'I'm Bob the Builder' and the practitioner nearby replied, 'Hello Bob'. Jon pointed to Winston and said,' Two Bob the Builders'. Rosie, who was at a nearby table, pointed to the hard hat and said, 'That's a real one'. A conversation followed about Jon's brother who had a woolly Bob the Builder hat for the winter. The two boys continued building their constructions with the blocks, singing the Bob the Builder song.

In Poplar Play Charlotte and Alric (both three years old) were playing with wooden trains and small blocks. I was sitting close by and Charlotte opened up the conversation with me. She wanted to show me her new socks. I expressed interest and listened but Charlotte carried on the conversation with connected comments. She started with, 'These are my new socks' (she showed me them), 'I bought them in John Lewis with my mum'. Then, 'We bought five socks'. Counting, partly on her fingers, Charlotte recalled three of the five types of sock they had bought. She then announced, 'And we bought tights for Mum'. Charlotte said, 'I have new slippers. They have special lights on' and she indicated where by running her finger round the edge of her shoes. I made a comment that, 'There aren't any lights on your shoes' and Charlotte corrected me, 'They are trainers' (they were). Alric appeared to have been listening and showed me his footwear, explaining, 'These are trainers too'.

Three-year-olds are usually able to adjust their language depending on the purpose of communication, activity, mood and the listener. They vary tone and emphasis to convey feelings like excitement. Three-year-olds are confident in the pattern of asking questions as well as replying to them. They use question words, like 'What?', 'Where?', 'When?' and often a regular 'Why?'. But they also convey questioning by the tone in their voice. Some three-year-olds pose questions that make you think, either because you're not sure of the answer or the best way to word your reply.

For example

In New River Green Rosie (three years) was in the middle of doing the jigsaw, when she pointed, to direct my attention to a nearby display where there was writing in a non-English alphabet. She talked a pretend language and told me, 'I'm talking a different language'. She smiled and did some more pretend non-English. She then returned to the jigsaw. There was no sense of making fun of any other language, just an understanding that there were languages other than her own and that they sounded completely different.

Three-year-olds are making the move into language as a tool and a means to handle abstract ideas. When three-year-olds are learning new ideas, they still need a concrete situation in which to ground the idea. But their questions show how, with more familiar ideas or close conceptual links, they can explore through language alone.

Three-year-olds are gaining understanding that words can stand in for real objects. For instance, two-year-olds who are asked, 'What is a ball?' assume that the adult questioner is confused about what a ball looks like and will point to a picture or find a ball to show and demonstrate. Three-year-olds increasingly understand that this question, as worded, means 'Tell me something about a ball' and will make comments like, 'It bounces' or 'I play tennis with my ball'.

Rising threes and many three-year-olds need personal conversation. They may manage an active group time with songs and stories, especially with an adept adult storyteller and props. They are too young for much in the way of exploration of ideas and issues in group activities like circle time. A spontaneous conversation that develops around the lunch or dough table can be a useful opportunity. But three-year-olds usually experience difficulty with group communication. They want to explore their own perspective and experience.

For example

In New River Green the children gathered in a group after the end of lunch. There were 18 children (three- and four-year-olds) and they were fidgety; not badly behaved, just being young children doing a bit of poking and touching. Their movements were a timely reminder that sitting still very close to each other is hard for this age group, and they had just come from sitting at the lunch table.

The practitioner was wise and swiftly moved from the possibility of a story to some songs. She said in a friendly way, 'I think we're all too restless for a story. We'll have some songs.' A child suggested 'Bob the Builder' and the practitioner countered with, 'We need to move. I think we need a song we can move to.' She started 'Leo the Lion', a song with lots of movement, singing from loud to very quiet and then loud again. The children were pleased and wanted to 'do it again!' and then a third time. They followed with several rounds of 'Heads, shoulders, knees and toes'.

The children were happy and enthused. They had an enjoyable group time, with no nagging and then headed off for outdoors or other activities as they chose.

Awareness of the written word

Many three-year-olds are aware that language comes in a written form. Experience from their families and group settings can support children to build this understanding bit by bit, with enthusiasm and a 'can do' outlook. There are no advantages, and considerable potential disadvantages, in pushing three-year-olds into written word recognition or handwriting exercises.

Each of the examples below are from family life. They are a strong reminder of how much children learn at home. Your role is often to acknowledge with parents how much they have done and are still doing to contribute directly to their children's early literacy. Parents may discount their involvement because they feel only 'educational experts' could be supporting literacy. You might encourage some parents to be more involved with their three-year-olds, using books and stories. But many parents just need their efforts recognised; they are already supporting their children in appropriate ways.

For example

Three-year-olds, with happy experiences of books, can have already built skills that are vital, developmentally appropriate building blocks for literacy.

- ■ Georgia (described by Cath Arnold) at rising three has made the connection between written words and songs, as well as adding extras that were meaningful to her. At two years and nine months Georgia sang Christmas carols to her grandmother, turning the page of the song book accurately as she sang. Then Georgia began to add the phrase, 'at the hotel' at the end of each rhyme. Her grandmother asked, 'Where did the hotel come from?' and Georgia explained, 'At the wedding'. The family was going to a wedding and would stay overnight in a hotel.

- Alice at three years (described by Robin Campbell) commented on and asked questions about many of her favourite books, although some she preferred to hear in silence. She liked repeat readings of books and had memorised parts of stories, joining in with whoever was reading to her. Alice recognised some words in her story books. She played at reading to herself, her toy animals and to her baby sister. Alice liked stories but was also beginning to understand that there were different kinds of books. At three and a half she described a gazetteer of maps as, 'It's a which way you're going book'.

- Drew (my son) at just three years of age was very enthusiastic about books. He had enjoyed stories and looking at books since babyhood, both with us and by accessing books as he wished from his own low shelf. At three years he knew much of his 'Goldilocks' book by heart, some of the long Thomas the Tank Engine stories and much of 'Oliver Button is a sissy'. He liked to tell us the story, turning the pages accurately as he moved along. Drew said he was 'reading' to us. He showed clear signs of saying and practising newly bought books, so that he soon wanted to recount the story. Drew had enthusiasm for books about things that interested him, as well as stories.

Three-year-olds can really enjoy books but storytelling is oral communication as well. Three-year-olds, who have been encouraged, can sometimes recount their own stories of what they have done and of interesting events. Confident three-year-olds and rising threes will sometimes fill in the gap, when they do not know a word, with 'this' and 'that' or expansive gestures.

Three-year-olds have often also started to explore mark making and they create meaningful curves, lines and separate early symbols, some of which may be recognisable as close to letters. They can have worked out that writing says something and want to have a try themselves, especially imitating older siblings and adults whom they see writing. Three-year-olds will often make pretend lists, want to write their name and show that they tell the difference between their drawing and what they call their writing. All that is needed is a supportive environment, easy access to writing materials and respectful adult interest for what children tell you is their shopping list or a note for the milkman.

Three-year-olds are not helped by being rushed to copying exercises with paper and pencil. Their physical skills build up gradually and they need plenty of relaxed practice for the co-ordination of vision and the physical movements that writing demands.

Researcher/practitioners like Sally Goddard Blythe have identified that large physical movements are just as important as fine movements. Three- and four-year-olds need to feel confident in their whole bodies and be able to respond to the physical messages of movement. Excessive and early writing practice is more likely to cramp children's fine movements. Yet, large movements, such as circling arms when playing with streamers or ribbons can build a firm basis. Children gain hand and eye control and strengthen muscles through confident use of tools in different kinds of indoor and outdoor activities.

For example

Three-year-olds who have had relaxed and playful practice show an awareness of the written word and enthusiastic mark making that is clearly meaningful to the individual children.

- At just over three years of age (3:2) Georgia accidentally drew an M and called out to her mother, 'Mummy me did Donalds', meaning McDonald's. From early three to three and half years, Georgia enjoyed drawing many curved symbols that she said were her writing. She copied her mother's writing of her younger brother's name, Harry. Georgia wanted to know why the written 'Mum' and

'Colette' (her mother's name) looked different. (It is obvious to us, but from Georgia's perspective why should the written version not be the same. Her mother looked the same whether she was called Mum or Colette.) Georgia also wrote what she said were tickets and distributed them. She wrote shopping lists and 'read' out the items.

■ Alice, at three years old, made a difference between her drawing and what she called her 'writing'. She recognised what was writing and wanted to know what words said, including captions on the television. She recognised some key logos from her everyday life, both in and out of their normal context. Alice recognised a few letters, named them and tried to write her own name.

■ Tanith at just two years imitated her older brother in asking us what specific written words said. At this age she confused written letters with numbers; she believed all the marks 'said something'. At just turned three years of age, Tanith (who at that age was known by her first name, Zoe) wanted to have a go at writing her own name, just as Drew (then five years old) was able to do. Since Tanith had asked, we showed her and let her try in her own way. She, by now, recognised her own name written down. She was still confused about the difference between letters and numbers. Ten months later, with no pressure at all, she was able to write her own name clearly and liked to do this on her drawings. She had now worked out that letters were not the same as numbers; they told you something different.

Anne Hughes and Sue Ellis (*Writing it Right*, Scottish Consultative Council on the Curriculum) point out that the major difference between early years settings and primary school is the balance between:

• **responding** to young children when they choose to do meaningful mark making or early writing and

• **recruiting** children into writing following a shared agenda in the group.

Primary school teachers do more recruiting because of the different staff-child ratio and demands of the curriculum, but also because the children are older. The balance for early years practitioners should be much more on responding to the explorations that three-, and four-year-olds, want to make and the way they choose to apply their skills. Helpful adults can then support and extend the child's emerging understanding. Early years practitioners can undermine children learning to be writers, when those adults believe they should mainly recruit three- and four-year-olds into worksheet copying and tracing letters.

Anne Hughes and Sue Ellis distinguish six broad themes around 'becoming a writer' for three-and four-year-olds and show that this process is as much about children understanding the whole writing business as the technical skills of making letters and words. The children, and adults in their support, need to take time to explore in many different ways:

• What writing looks like

• How to make letters and symbols

• That writing is used for a whole range of purposes in real life, for thinking and communicating

• That people enjoy writing

• That writing gives status and power (in a positive way) to the writer

• That writing lets you keep ideas for ever and tell others about them even when you haven't met

You might like to look at your own practice over the days and weeks and identify the different ways in which you support these different and equally important kinds of literacy learning.

Mathematical Development

Adults can only give effective support for young children's mathematical understanding if they have a firm grasp of how the ideas develop for three-year-olds. Practitioners and parents are often focused far more on 'completed' mathematical ideas that make sense to them, rather than homing in on all the little steps along the way. Another issue with mathematics is that some adults (parents and practitioners) are profoundly uneasy about this area of learning because of their own unpleasant memories of 'school maths'. Childhood emotions of confusion, the dread of making mistakes and feeling stupid can get in the way of being a helpful adult.

An interest in numbers and counting

The ideas and research of Jean Piaget, a Swiss developmental psychologist, have had a strong influence on early years practice in the UK. The exciting aspect of his work was that Piaget showed young children to be active learners, making sense of what was around them and exploring in a deliberate way. The drawback was that Piaget tended to describe and define children younger than five or six years in terms of what they could not do, in this case that they could not conserve quantity. What Piaget meant was that young children did not yet understand that the number of items stayed the same, regardless of how those items were laid out - whether in a row, a pile or any other arrangement.

In Piaget's experiments, children seemed to believe that the answer to 'How many?' varied with the layout of items. Three- and four-year-olds often concluded that a widely spaced row of items had 'more' than a closely packed one. But, as Margaret Donaldson and her team (initially at Edinburgh during the 1970s) have so effectively shown, part of the thinking being demonstrated is that young children are more likely to give this opinion when adults have made the change and ask the question. Young children tend to conclude that something must be different, otherwise why would an adult ask them this kind of question. Three-year-olds are thinking about how the world works, what changes and what does not. There is also considerably more to the understanding of number than conservation of quantity. Three- and four-year-olds can develop a good practical grasp of number in ordinary situations and continue to learn the more subtle aspects.

The unhelpful practical application of Piaget's research was the belief that children must grasp the idea of conservation of quantity before they can develop the concept of number. More recent research, and

observation of natural (non-experimental) home and nursery settings, shows that this is a narrow and unrealistic view of children's power of thought. The influence of Piaget also led to some dismissive views of children's enthusiasm for counting, and parents' excitement about their young children's ability.

Such skills were, and sometimes still are, dismissed as 'just rote learning' or 'only parotting numbers'. But children count with meaning and understanding and these skills build real mathematical understanding. So, in this area of learning, probably even more so than some of the other areas, early years practitioners need to tune in to children's current level of understanding. Three-year-olds are very likely to:

• Have some understanding of spoken number and counting, and grasp a range of practical applications that make sense in everyday life. The pattern for three-year-olds will be individual and reflect their experience so far at home and in any setting.

• They may recognise that numbers are also written but may confuse the number and letter system, assuming it is all one meaningful set of symbols that 'say' something.

Food for thought

Dorothy Caddell (1998) explains clearly how learning within family life is so appropriate for supporting children's early mathematical ideas and practice. Early years practitioners need to be aware that mathematical understanding is best supported in social interaction through daily routines and events and playful games involving number. Home-like activities are more appropriate for children's learning than worksheets and the rush to abstract written number. Parents are often fully engaged in exactly the right kinds of activity, but believe they cannot be supporting maths, because this is an expert's task.

Practitioners can alert parents to the excellent support they are already offering or guide those families who are not helping their three-year-olds.

For example

One meaning that numbers have for young children is age: a matter of some importance when you are three or four years old. Attentive adults who listen to three-year-olds' comments can gain a fascinating insight into young children's thinking and the ways in which numbers and other mathematical concepts begin to make sense to them.

■ When Georgia became three years old, she counted one, two, three and said she was three. The number three was a descriptive word for her as an individual. Georgia had a name that belonged to her and an age. Some months later her friend Stephanie had her fourth birthday and Georgia was puzzled as to how her close friend could be four and she was not. She asked similar questions repeatedly about why Stephanie would be four before herself. Her mother explained several times that it was about who was born first. Around this time Georgia recognised that adults had an age as well but had some difficulty with what number this might be. Her first guess was to ask her mother, 'You are eleventeen?' then she guessed six, followed by twenty.

■ Young children often relate numbers to age. A three-year-old in one nursery class looked seriously at me during a conversation we were having about birthdays and said, 'Did you know, you have to be three before you're allowed to be four?' Some children ask questions about why ages are put on labels of children's clothes but not on adults'. It is a symbol of the confusing message to children that age in number is intermingled with size, as in 'When you're big, you'll go to school'.

Being a helpful adult

Dorothy Caddell offers a useful description of the strands of number learning for young children, all of which work when children can see adults using numbers for a real purpose, not abstractions. She suggests that children can then learn through daily routines and ordinary events that:

- Numbers give information (telephone numbers, prices, how old you are.)

- Numbers help us to make decisions (which bus to catch, the right size of clothes, the temperature to bake a cake)

- Numbers can be fun, part of playful activities (counting before you seek in hide and seek, number rhymes)

- Numbers can be used to impress (when children say they have 'hundreds and hundreds' of something, children may use their age to impress)

You might like to observe in your setting or family home and see in what ways children can grasp all these uses of number over the days and weeks and through ordinary activities.

In a similar way to supporting writing (see page 29), genuinely helpful adults respond to the three-year-olds' interest in what they can recognise as early maths, rather than trying to recruit young children into completing mathematical activities such as worksheets, that risk making little sense to them.

■ In my own household we had related conversations to which Drew returned over several weeks, when he had not long turned four. He wanted to unravel, at his own pace and through his chosen questions, the interplay between what age you were, how big you were and what did not change over time, like whether you were a boy or girl, a brother or a sister. For more detail on this example see *What Does it Mean to be Four?*, page 40.

■ Tanith at just two years recognised that written symbols said something, but did not have the understanding to distinguish between letters and numbers. She liked to say, 'One, two, three, four', but without reference to anything in particular. At her developmental check when two, she tried to use a pencil to copy the shapes, as she had seen Drew do in his four-year-old check, a short while previously. She looked worried and said to me, 'Can't do it' and I reassured her that the doctor did not expect her to manage what her brother had done; Drew was two years older. At two and half years Tanith could finger point to count a small number of objects. She liked to count up to five and sometimes made it to ten. At just over three years, Tanith could reliably finger point to count objects like books or bricks, up to five or six or more. She was confident counting up to ten, but liked some help with an adult voice joining in from ten to twenty.

■ In New River Green Centre Rosie (three years old) wanted me to look at the tank of tropical fish close by where we were sitting, doing a jigsaw. Rosie chose spontaneously to count the fish. First she counted up to eight and got confused. After a short gap she counted accurately up to 15, pointing to individual fish as she progressed. We agreed that the counting was hard because the fish kept moving.

Three-year-olds need plenty of practice getting familiar with number order: that you count up in the same pattern each time. We know that six follows five each time when you are counting higher numbers but we learned this fact, it is not obvious at the outset. Three-year-olds are in the process of learning, and some have grasped that, if you want five bricks or three spades, you stop counting at that number, rather than go on and on until you run out of the numbers you know. Three-year-olds learn through watching adults or their peers who demonstrate that it is useful to count by finger pointing or physically moving the bricks or spades to see when they have 'enough'.

Understanding and using concepts

Three-year-olds show that they understand a range of early mathematical ideas but the pattern is very individual. Helpful adults at home and in a group setting need to listen to what children say and watch what they do in order to grasp what interested the children and where their learning has taken them so far. When adults insist on following their own plan to promote mathematical understanding, there is a strong risk that many of the children will not grasp what you are talking about, because your words fail to connect with the ideas they have already. Helpful adults add a little to what interests a child and recognise that, with a well-resourced environment, three-year-olds are grasping mathematical ideas.

- Three-year-olds are aware of basic ideas of size and relative size of objects, although probably with the handy general terms of 'big' and 'little'.

- Three-year-olds make a great deal of sense of these abstract ideas through the medium of physical movement, the opportunities presented by outdoor play and involvement in daily routines. Height, fit, too big for, too high for, just right – all these ideas often make sense because of playful experiences around climbing equipment, constructions, creative explorations with dough and pretend play.

- Three-year-olds can have an understanding of height and weight through climbing, looking up and carrying, long before they are ready to grasp abstract measurement of these ideas.

- Through direct experience and use of their own chosen questions, three-year-olds begin to unravel some of the intriguing confusions. This pattern will be individual and helpful adults listen, watch and answer the questions that children ask. Some three-year-olds want to unpack the idea of age and number (see the example on page 31). Some wonder about 'bigness' and if something that is big will also be heavy, difficult to lift.

For example

Rising threes and three-year-olds make sense of mathematical concepts from situations that are meaningful to them. Money is a complicated concept and it takes children time to grasp all the different aspects of how money and the different coinage works. Yet this understanding can start very young. Shapes and even fractions begin to make sense in an activity that children can touch and work upon in their own way.

■ Georgia at nearly two and a half liked playing with tickets and coins. She gave her mum some coins and waited to get some back. In her play she often announced, 'Pay the man' and she called a 20 pence coin a 'choo choo', a direct link to the experience that this coin was needed to pay for a ride on the toy train at the supermarket. At three years and nine months Georgia was adept at counting, showing an understanding that you count each object in turn and stop with the last. The final number is the tally. She had organised items in a line up to now and then announced, 'I'm going to make a circle' using coins and, 'I'm going to count them now'. The circle was more difficult and Georgia forgot where she had started.

■ In New River Green Jake (three years old) had flattened out his portion of red dough and was now carefully cutting into the dough with a pair of scissors. As he cut, he informed me, 'This is a pancake cut in half and now it's going to be cut in half again.' After some careful cutting Jake worked on merging the portions back into one pile, saying, 'I flatten it down, I want it to go on the other one'.

■ In Poplar Play Centre, Alric (three years) and Michael (two years) were busy at the table with paper and 2-d shapes. The children could draw round the outside of any shape, but also inside to create an inner square, triangle and so on. Michael was keen but sometimes he drew inside the shape, rather like colouring in and sometimes he managed to hold a felt tip to the inside edge. Alric had learned to hold the shape firm and could draw an inside line with confidence. He moved the triangle shape to make a series of drawn shapes on his paper, holding his felt tip in a fist grip. Alric looked pleased and showed his paper to the practitioner, 'Look at the triankles (how he says the word). I made them all!' The practitioner said the word triangle correctly for him and admired his work.

Pretend play is another context in which three-year-olds test out and use what adults can recognise as early mathematical concepts. Three-year-olds show complex pretend play, often with long sequences, some of which change without apparent reason (from the adult perspective). They use all available props, not only dressing-up clothes and items that adults envisage as pretend play materials. They use doll's house size figures and small world play such as a farm and animals. Three-year-olds enjoy a home corner or other flexible areas of a nursery but they do not need extensive props. In a family home a sofa can easily become a pretend café, a ship in a storm or a safe haven from monsters.

Children's involvement in domestic routines is also valuable, whether in a family home or group setting whose team sensibly values such times. Direct experience through hands-on activities is important for three-year-olds. They cannot grapple with ideas that do not connect with their experience or what is in front of them at this moment.

For example

In New River Green, Jake (three years old) was playing with the Duplo on his own. I sat nearby and he moved across to the train set. Jake talked out loud about what he was doing with the trains. His words were partly addressed to me but also seemed to work as a monologue guiding and planning his play.

Jake gathered up most of the carriages and the trains, 'I need all of these. Do you know why? Because I'm going to make two trains. And this one is going this way and that one is going this way.' He indicated with his hand the different directions around the laid out track, which had a sloped section and several cross-over points.

Jake built the trains, adding carriages and took care to line up the magnetic dots that held the parts together to make a sequence. He showed understanding that the magnetism worked in one direction only. If the first fit did not hold the carriages, then he confidently switched them around so that it did work.

Jake took care guiding trains around the track. He had built trains with several carriages and getting them round the bends was not easy. There were crashes and trains tipping off the rails. Jake commented and explained to me as he played, 'He's got to pull the one he banged' and 'Do you know how he's going to rescue him? If he does this like that' and demonstrated as he talked.

Jake explained how he put the trains together, 'This will be the last carriage' and concentrated on fixing trains and carriages, lining them up on the track, moving them round and re-setting them as they tumbled off quite easily. In the end he commented about the scenario, 'The trucks are very grumpy because they've been here a lot of years' and then, 'The carriages have to hide in the dark tunnel because of the bumps from the other train'.

- Look also at the example on page 54 of Rosie and Ben to see how mathematical ideas flow through their long pretend play sequence in the block area as well as many other creative ideas.

Three-year-olds are often aware of different kinds of size and relative size and shape: what will fit and what will not, what is big, small, too big and about right for the task in hand. Rising threes and three-year-olds build their understanding through direct experience, plenty of hands-on practice and appropriate sharing of words and phrases by helpful adults. Three-year-olds continue to learn by building on what they already know.

There is no need to rush children on to precise language for size, shape or measurements and certainly not to restrict the adult view of mathematical learning to two-dimensional worksheet experiences. Three-year-olds sometimes enjoy handling shapes (see the example on page 33) but they also need the three-dimensional experiences. Three years do not learn about shape from a 'shape table' any more than they grasp colour from a 'colour of the week'. In fact, such a focus does not make much sense until young children have learned about the different kinds of shape and visually tuned into colour through plenty of hands-on practice and conversation.

The passing of time and 'time for ...'

Three-year-olds do not understand clock time. It is not unusual that six- or seven-year-olds are still confused with telling the time. It is a complicated idea and children now face many different kinds of timepiece: analogue and digital. But time is much more than clocks and watches. In a reasonably predictable day and week three-year-olds understand about the sequences of what follows what: a practical and meaningful application of the concept of time.

Three-year-olds are learning how to manage their own time as they make choices about what they will do now and later (see the example on page 20). Rising threes and three-year-olds often have some idea of a few days of the week because something special happens on those days. Three-year-olds do not yet have a clear idea of the pattern of the named days. But perhaps Tuesday has meaning because it is when a favourite programme is on the television or Friday is the day we pay the milkman.

Time measures like five minutes or half an hour do not mean anything to three-year-olds, and not much more to four- or five-year-olds. Yet three-year-olds can make sense of 'We can do one more market stall and then we need to go back to nursery for our lunch'.

For example

Three-year-olds are often confused by timepieces and show curiosity that helpful adults can meet, without holding unrealistic expectations of very young children. Over the years I have observed three- and four-year-olds be interested and show understanding in different ways.

- Three-year-olds are often interested in what a clock or watch says. They may be intrigued by different kinds of timepiece, for instance that a timepiece may be on the wall, on someone's wrist and even round their neck on a chain. As adults we know that these are all different kinds of watches but children do not know this yet.

- When doing observation, I sometimes use a stopwatch. Three- and four-year-olds have often homed in on my timepiece and wanted to know 'What time is it?' Some have realised that the movements on the face are a bit odd and asked, 'Is it a watch?' or 'What have you got there?' It has then been a challenging task to explain in simple words that my stopwatch tells me about time passing, how long something has taken rather than what time it is.

- Three-year-olds can begin to understand the passing of time and ways to indicate when 'time is up'. Nurseries and playgroups often use a sand timer, and sometimes have several that measure different amounts of time passing. These timers are often used for practical reasons, such as a fair approach to turn taking on the bikes or other favourite equipment. Such a system is then usually run by the children themselves, three-year-olds and fours.

- In my own family, by three and four years my children had grasped the idea of using the timer on the cooker to measure a small amount of time. One use was to guide a short calm-down time when everyone had got rather fraught. But my children also spontaneously suggested the timer when I said I wanted a short while with my feet up before I was ready to play again. They required a particular number of minutes that were then set on the timer (and which passed very quickly!). This activity became known in our family as 'setting the pinger'.

Food for thought

Three-year-olds often like counting and they enjoy relaxed practice in situations that they want to explore (see the examples on pages 26 and 32). Supportive adults watch, listen and offer a bit of help when appropriate, without taking over. There are plenty of opportunities that arise spontaneously through play. The other important source of meaningful early mathematics arises from the involvement of children in domestic routines, at home and in a group setting.

Laying the table, tidying up, making choices about how a setting is organised - all of these activities are valuable opportunities for practical maths, as well as a sound basis for children's social and emotional development. I have observed excellent early years practice in settings where practitioners value the caring routines. But this perspective is not always shared when other adults take on what I would call 'educational tunnel vision'. An excessively formal approach to early learning dismisses the routines as 'just care', as times when learning cannot possibly be occurring.

I was first alerted to this problem by the manager of a day nursery whose team valued the routines and undertook a wide range of meaningful practical maths through these activities. The person who carried out their Ofsted inspection for the four-year-old funding (prior to the merging of the inspections) got up abruptly as soon as the morning session moved towards the lunch-time routine saying, 'I'll take my break now. Nothing is going to happen until this afternoon' and promptly disappeared. The nursery team was highly irritated to see in their report a criticism that the inspector had seen 'no sign of early number activities'; he had chosen to absent himself from the part of the day in which children did a great deal of counting, sorting and sharing out.

Knowledge and Understanding of the World

If children are to extend their understanding, they need experiences and reactions from adults that support their curiosity. Look at your practice to check:

- Who asks the questions? Children show their natural curiosity through comments and asking questions. They will learn most by getting answers to the questions they want to ask today, right this moment.

- Adult questions can be useful, so long as they are open-ended and speculative (see page 26). The more closed the questions, the more a child is put in a 'Do you know this?' situation.

- Three-year-olds can be enthusiastic about the illustrations in books and images from television, but they need to explore in the real environment as well. Then they make connections between what they can see locally and what they find in books. Hands-on experiences and direct observations also help children to build the understanding that supports distinctions between what they can see locally and what is in books or videos 'but not round here'.

Three-year-olds are interested and ready to be intrigued. Unless their confidence has already been dented or their experiences very limited indeed, children in this age group are only too happy to explore, touch, feel, smell and generally find out about their immediate environment. A great deal of finding out about their world requires that children are able to move and have easy access to the outdoors.

For example

I spent an enjoyable morning with three- and four-year-olds in St Peter's nursery class. This team was thoughtful about the experiences they provided for the children and the whole aim of their planning was to be able as adults to act flexibly within each day. For instance, within the morning a small group of children found a large spider in the outdoor sandpit. The practitioner who was in the garden with the children responded immediately to their excitement. She spent time bent down with them watching the spider and chatting, but following the children's lead. It was an excellent example of following the moment and the children's fascinated interest.

Later in the morning there was a more planned event to extend the children's understanding of how the local neighbourhood worked. The milkman, who had delivered to the nursery for many years, was on his last day and had been invited to join the end-of-morning group. The children were interested, some asked questions and the comments illustrated that young children are, and remain for some time, rather perplexed by the adult world of work.

Moving outwards from themselves

Three-year-olds are focused on themselves as a natural part of their development (see also page 10). Their learning extends from their own perspective outwards in time and place.

- Three-year-olds begin to grasp what can much later be 'history' from exploration of their own personal time lines and through learning about their family and the background of their friends, in a non-intrusive way. Three-year-olds are often intrigued to realise that grown-ups, such as familiar early years practitioners, also had a childhood and have mummies and daddies.

- A sense of what will later be 'geography' builds from three-year-olds' general knowledge of the local neighbourhood and journeys that make sense to them, because the trip has personal significance. Three-year-olds are interested in and keen to make sense of their local routes. They begin to build mental maps, like 'how we get to the library' and simple links between different locations. This development is much more effective when young children walk than travel as passengers in a car.

- Three-year-olds have only a vague idea of distance. 'How far?' in measured miles is often confused for some years with how long it takes you to get there, which in turn depends on the mode of transport. But young children can gain an understanding and want to chat about their street, their shops and park, round the corner, a long walk away or as far as Gran's house.

- Globes and maps do not make sense yet to three-year-olds. They enjoy three-dimensional small world play but the two-dimensional map representation is confusing at the start and does not connect with children's first-hand experience.

- Three-year-olds may begin to get an idea when the map concept links directly to a personal experience (see the example on page 14). A local map can make sense when you use it with children as you walk the route. Listen to children's questions, they will maybe notice that things they see in front of them are not all on the map.

- A sense of social group and culture can build over time. But adults need to be wary about trying to go too fast to extend three-year-olds' understanding into unfamiliar groups, when they do not yet have a firm grasp of what makes their own identity (see also page 13).

Being a helpful adult

- Children need the time to look and to ponder. Sometimes they do not want to talk about what they are experiencing. Adults need to look and listen as well. Now is not always the time to give information or ask questions. Children benefit from seeing that you find this sight interesting or perplexing.

- Details matter to children but you have to listen to know what details are significant to this child or small group. You may have taken the children to see the ducklings in the park, but what the children want to talk about on the walk back is why people throw their rubbish into the lake.

All about me

Young scientists and technicians

Three-year-olds are curious and, unless their confidence has been seriously dented, they are not worried about what they do not yet know. Their curiosity, skills of observation, and openness to knowledge are a firm basis for a scientific outlook. Even children's pleasure in imaginative play offers a strong support since much scientific thinking requires something of a 'let's pretend' leap.

Three-year-olds are interested in many aspects of what will become early science. They can be fascinated by the flowers, trees and creatures in their local environment. They are keen to explore natural materials like sand, earth, peat, water and created mixes like playdough. They are interested in and often puzzled by the weather. They like hands-on activities such as cooking. Three-year-olds are also interested in bodies and bodily functions and their questions show that they want to unpack some of the more puzzling events. The pattern is again very individual and families may have the more private conversations, especially about babies.

For example

Everyday experiences support children's understanding of how the natural world works.

- Georgia at three years and four months was intrigued to see her father put a tub of margarine in the bin. She asked, 'Why are you throwing it away?' Her father explained, 'Because the fridge was up too high and it's frozen'. The bottom of the tub was covered in a sheet of ice and Georgia commented, 'That's why you making glass.' Georgia was very interested in water, watering plants and what effect water had on other materials. One day, she said, 'It's raining, my slide's wet!' Her mother suggested, 'You'd better slide down it to dry it' and Georgia countered with, 'No - I can't because my bum will get wet.'

Three-year-olds are intrigued to use their physical skills to make things of their own choosing and to solve simple problems in their play (see the examples on pages 46 and 53). Even young children use their skills of observation to grasp how objects and appliances work in a practical way. Adult support to extend three-year-old knowledge needs to work from the children's current understanding. Young children get lost the more they are forced to process ideas they scarcely understand and to deal with ideas or words lacking a familiar context.

Some early years settings have experienced a strong pressure to introduce and use computers, even with under threes. Such a development is not necessarily developmentally sound (see also the discussion on page 40). However, the Foundation Stage guidance is in no way requiring that young children must spend time on computers. The relevant section of this area of learning is about Information and Communication Technology (ICT). This term includes computers but is much broader. Three-year-olds can already be interested in everyday technology and able to use some domestic appliances.

- Three-year-olds can be aware of high street technology such as the pedestrian crossing signals with the red and green figures, traffic lights and check-outs at supermarkets.

- They have often noticed automatic doors and the security CCTV screens in some shopping areas or train and bus stations.

- Three-year-olds are often interested in home ICT: the controls on the washing machine or dishwasher, how to work the video and audio tape machine.

- Three-year-olds often integrate everyday technology into their play and their pretend play themes. They show an accurate grasp of how the real thing works.

For example

Creative use of the computer area is shown in an observation made in the Thomas Coram Early Childhood Centre and reported as part of the Mosaic consultation project.

The children were a mixed group of three- and four-year-olds. Gaby, who was a major player in this scenario taking place close to the computer table, was three years old at the time. Gaby had a baby (a doll) who wasn't well. She lay the doll on the mouse mat for the computer and used the mouse to pump the baby's chest and make her better: 'Daddy is coming home soon. The baby is OK. She is moving'. More children joined in. There were eight children involved in this game at one point. Two of the boys were told to be babies too. Gaby's baby was Gary and Meryl's baby was John. 'Let me change your nappy darling,' said Gaby to Gary.' (page 13)

Being a helpful adult

The DATEC project (Developmentally Appropriate Technology for Early Childhood) highlights key issues that are important if adults are to be genuinely helpful.

- The project team stresses the great importance of a broad approach to everyday technology, supporting children's steady ability to work the tools of ICT. In order to promote this learning, early years practitioners and parents need to be aware and confident in their own use of ICT, not thinking that learning is restricted to computers.

- There are good opportunities for broad learning when ICT is made available to support children's pretend play with real or pretend appliances and when ICT is easy to access in support of any existing activities and projects of interest to the children.

- The whole message for three-year-olds is that of choice and steadily learning that the tools and equipment of ICT are part of everyday life and not restricted to the computer area or table.

- Adults need to take a careful look at what any software offers. Will it really support children's learning? Look for ways to integrate what can be done on the computer with any work elsewhere in the setting.

- The DATEC team advises strongly against using time on the computer as a reward or withdrawing this opportunity as a consequence of disruptive behaviour. The computer should be treated like any other resource in your setting and not as something special.

Adult support for this area of learning can build on what interests three-year-olds. Theorists like Jean Piaget did not talk much about technology, because the world was different in the first half of the twentieth century. But young children will, of course, be curious about their social world and especially interested in the tools of the adult world and adult activities. They have skills of looking, imitating and fine finger movement. They are not daunted by technology when young; it is just something else of interest to poke and explore.

For example

Jannik Beyer and Lone Gammelhoft in *Autism and Play* (Jessica Kingsley) give the example of Lukas, who is not autistic, to demonstrate how play develops usually in the early years. The example shows very well how even toddlers are interested in and begin to understand the ICT that is a normal feature in many family homes.

At five months, Lukas played with the television remote control. He put it in his mouth and knocked it to the floor. The remote was an object without special significance. But by eight months, Lukas would sit with the remote control and point it at everybody and everything. He did not understand how it controlled the television, but Lukas had worked out that the remote was a valuable object, having watched his older siblings squabble over the right to use it. Within only one more month, Lukas had worked out how to find and press the red button as he pointed the remote control towards the television. He switched off in the middle of his older sister's favourite programme and squealed happily at his achievement. By 22 months, Lukas had understood fully that the remote control operated the television. He now chose to pretend that it was something else. He ran around his home with the remote, sometimes held it to his ear and said 'loh'. He was pretending to speak on a mobile telephone.

For example

- My son Drew by just three years of age had observed my own activities in running my business out of the ground floor of our home. His younger sister and I were waiting in the hallway, with an adult friend and her four-year-old, to go out locally. Drew appeared at the top of the stairs holding his red toy telephone. He held up two fingers in a counting gesture and announced, 'I must just make two calls'. He then sat on the top step, holding the telephone and the receiver in an accurate grip, dialled and made two separate 'calls' with a serious look on his face. He then put the telephone on the floor and came down the stairs. As you can imagine, Drew had re-enacted exactly my own behaviour on other days, right down to my words and tone of voice.

- Rising threes and three-year-olds can be competent in managing familiar technology and they assume that similar equipment works in the same way. I had to extricate an audio tape from my video machine (successfully in the end) after two-year-old Benjamin had confidently slotted in his story tape. Benjamin was adept at working an audio cassette at home and had assumed my video was the same kind of appliance. He was not behaving badly; Benjamin had just generalised from what he knew.

There is no rush to get rising threes and three-year-olds on computers. There is further discussion of this issue in *What Does it Mean to be Four?* on page 42. The main areas of concern are that:

- Young children need plenty of experience with three-dimensional materials and hands-on activities.
- They need to value their own drawings and constructions and not risk the sense that they can never produce something as neatly and quickly as the software package. Creativity, physical skills, exploration and real planning can be diminished.
- Some computer software directs children towards expecting quick reactions and learning to be intolerant of waiting and pondering.

Physical Development

Physical development is just as important for children's learning and their emotional well-being as the other five broad areas of learning. The guidance to the Foundation Stage is very clear that there are no 'first division' and 'second division' areas within the six. Yet there does seem to be a risk that children's physical development is undervalued by some early years practitioners and parents in favour of what seem like the more important 'intellectual' areas.

Why physical development matters so much

Helen Bee (in *The Developing Child*, Longman, 1997) acknowledged that psychologists and child development researchers have largely ignored the importance of physical development. They have described the changes, but without recognition of the meaning for children's personal and social world. In child psychology, the development of communication and cognition has attracted far more adult interest than physical development.

Yet children's physical development is important for their all-round development and well-being:

• Children's physical growth makes new behaviours possible. Lack of some skills within physical development can set a limit to current possibilities. Some limits are perfectly normal, for instance, young toddlers cannot easily pick up small objects. Young children can be impressive climbers and bikers but even six-year-olds cannot reliably hit balls with bats or throw balls through hoops, no matter how hard adults make them try. Some of the physical skills still need to develop through middle childhood.

• Children's growth determines their potential experiences within their everyday life. Independent mobility for a toddler creates an extended personal world in which they can make choices and take action on what they want to reach and handle. Three-year-olds who can manage to fasten and unfasten their own coat and shoes have more direct control about moving on to the next part of their day. Four-year-olds who can manhandle boxes and other recycled materials experience the satisfaction of announcing, 'We did this all on our own!'

• The many physical skills that support co-operative play also provide the context for social interaction and rich communication. Children enjoy doing activities together, planning and making something happen. Three-, four- and five-year-olds have more scope to develop these social skills when they are on the move. They can plan, carry out and then admire big-scale projects.

- Children's growth affects the responses of other people. Children who are smaller or larger than average, compared with their peers, often get treated differently by children and adults. All children need to learn the skills of co-ordination but being better co-ordinated or more 'clumsy' than your peers brings comment on children.

- Children's growth also affects their self-concept through a growing sense of their bodily image. Children notice how others react and what is said to them. Three-year-olds are unlikely to be sensitive as yet, unless they have been on the receiving end of very offhand remarks. But four and five years can begin to believe what others, adults or other children, say to them. Does the child feel clumsy, slow, big and gawky or lithe, nifty, a good runner or climber?

- Physical development and generous opportunity for activity also matters a great deal to support the often more valued intellectual areas such as literacy. Young children need to have had plenty of practice in all the different kinds of large and fine physical movements if they are to be ready and physically confident to manage writing and reading (see also page 28).

The importance of movement

Physical activity to support development and emotional well-being matters a great deal because young children are happy when they can move about. They show that they need space - indoors and outside. They are very capable of learning outside and the entire early years curriculum can be accessed using the outdoor spaces. Indeed, some aspects of the curriculum, such as Knowledge and Understanding of the World, cannot be effectively offered without generous outdoor access.

Enjoyable physical activity supports children's overall health. Active, physically busy children burn up their calories, work up a genuine appetite and enjoy their food. Physically active children are often able to rest fully, because they have been active during the daylight hours. Increased physical activity increases the blood flow to the brain. Children's mental alertness is often boosted by taking a break, and they concentrate more easily if they are allowed to move. In contrast, making children sit still and be quiet causes them to be more sluggish and less able to learn.

Physical activity helps children to build up strong muscles, suppleness in the joints and bone density. There is considerable concern in our society about inactive, lethargic children who have lost the motivation to play lively games, preferring passive activity, especially with excessive television or computer usage. Such habits are learned in early childhood. Babies and toddlers have a passion for movement and are keen to use all their current physical skills to the utmost. It takes active adult discouragement as well as a lack of easy-to-access activities to produce young 'couch potatoes'. In reasonably well resourced settings with easy access to the outdoors, three, four and five years are only too pleased to be 'runner beans' - Marjorie Ouvry's lovely phrase.

The worst combination is when children, who have learned habits of inaction and a preference for passive activities, have also been allowed to learn unhealthy eating habits: constant snacking and a poor range of food. In extreme cases, such a life style can lead to childhood obesity, and make children vulnerable to health problems usually associated with middle-aged adults, such as type two diabetes (late onset).

Healthy eating habits are partly about food and partly establishing the pattern of mealtimes, so that children experience what it is like to feel hungry, to satisfy that hunger and to feel full, at which point you stop eating. The serious disadvantage of letting children snack is that they do not build habits that food is for satisfying hunger pangs. Snacking, especially as an accompaniment to passive activities like watching television or videos, becomes just something that children do with their hands, another source of low level stimulation.

For example

Happy mealtimes build healthy eating habits. It is also noticeable that young children will often painlessly eat good quality food. Sometimes adults talk as if you have to persuade young children into eating fruit. In most cases, you just have to put it in front of young children.

- In Poplar Play, I sat at the lunch table and dessert was a bowl for each table of orange and melon chunks, cut into the right size for little hands. These bowls all emptied with no persuasion at all from the adults. The fruit was eaten with obvious relish at all the tables, along with some discussion on the three- and four-year-old table about what the fruit was called.

- I attended a fruit-tasting day at a local drop-in run by Brighton and Hove Playlink. The children were young, many of them just rising twos, and there was great enthusiasm for all the different kinds of fruit that had been bought for tasting. At the end I was sitting at a table with some of the mothers and one had a nearly two-year-old on her lap. The young boy was taking his time selecting fruit one piece at a time from the large bowl on the table. He would look carefully, move in with a finger and thumb movement to pick a piece. Then he held it up and looked questioningly towards his mother. She would tell him the name of the piece of fruit he had picked, he popped it in his mouth and then looked for his next bit.

Physical skills of three-year-olds

Young children build their skills and sense of physical confidence through practice, suitable equipment and the support of adults who keep them safe enough but avoid fussing with excessive, 'Watch out!' or 'You'll hurt yourself!'

For example

In Poplar Play there is a child-sized trampoline that offers a good springy quality with a bar for children to hold as they bounce up and down. During the first part of the morning children of different ages enjoyed this piece of equipment. Their activity showed individual differences as well as the developmental progress of the skills needed to work the trampoline.

- Jerome and Michael (both two years old) were on the trampoline together bouncing well. They called out, 'Bouncy, bouncy' as they went up and down, and their practitioner counted their bounces for them.

- Then Isobelle (not quite two years) and Jack (two and a half) had a go. The difference between these two children was striking. Isobelle looked as if she was enjoying herself going up and down but she was moved mainly by Jack's vigorous bouncing. Isobelle bent at the knees and tried to lift off, but for the time being, she had trouble co-ordinating for the bounce and both her feet stayed on the trampoline. Jack, slightly older, bent his knees and launched well for the bounce, with both his feet leaving the surface at the same time.

- Later in the morning, after toast, Jack was back on the trampoline with Tom (also two years old). They both bounced with great confidence, controlling their movements and, by holding onto the bar as well as good physical direction, avoiding crashing into each other. Jack showed that he could also manage an open-scissors movement of his legs within his jump before landing back on the material surface.

- Later in the same morning Kimberley (five years old) bounced energetically on the trampoline, counting accurately at the same time, first out loud - up to seven - and then almost under her breath. Kimberley was not counting her bounces but the count before she shouted, 'Coming ready or not' and headed off to find the other children playing hide and seek in the garden.

For example

In Poplar Play, Chloe (two years) and Charlotte (three years) were sitting on either side of a wooden rocking seat. They worked it efficiently together by movements of their whole body and still managed to sing at the same time. First of all they sang several rounds of, 'One, two, three, four, five, once I caught a fish alive' and then followed this song with an equally enthusiastic version of 'Row, row, row the boat'.

Later Jack (two years old) sat in the two-person rocker on his own. He was able to work the rocking motion, even without a partner. He chose not to hold on tight to the sides of the rocker and so slipped off the seat into the well of the rocker several times. Jack seemed to find this amusing. He laughed and readjusted each time and informed me, 'This is my boat'.

For example

In New River Green, four boys (mixed three- and four-year-olds) were very busy in the block area: a generous carpeted space with a large supply of wooden blocks, planks and shapes of different sizes. The boys were keenly building upright towers of the large open blocks. The aim was to build high, about as high as they could reach, and then push the tower over, so that the blocks fell in a jumbled line across the carpet. The collapse of each tower was greeted with outbursts of delighted chortling, followed by a flurry of re-building, with the boys working well together in full co-operation.

One early years practitioner sitting with another small group at a nearby table kept an eye on the builders, but in no way cramped their style or the noise level (which was not excessive). On a couple of occasions, she gave a calm reminder that the boys check there was nobody on the falling side of the blocks. There was space for this building and demolition activity and the practitioner let it flow. After a while, two of the boys left and the remaining two found themselves hard hats and returned to a different style of building (see the example on page 26.)

Helpful adults recognise and respect the hard work and practice that children need to apply in their physical development:

- Three-year-olds are still fine tuning most of the large and fine movements that we take for granted. They need space, encouragement and plenty of relaxed time to practice, to do it again as confidence grows.

- Generous use of movement helps children to gain confident balance and to be sensitive to the messages that their body sends through that movement.

- Fine physical skills require delicate, deliberate movements and the close co-ordination of senses like sight and hearing with the movement of limbs like hands.

- Large and fine movements need children to make judgements about where their hands and feet will go. Once they feel confident, then they do not need to take the time to look, but plenty of practice is required before movements look and feel automatic.

- Practice and fine tuning of large and fine movements involves cognitive as well as physical skills: of planning, recall and concentration. Adults need to recognise this and not behave as if children are only concentrating if they are sitting still. As Sally Goddard Blythe has well described, sitting still is the hardest movement of all to control. Three-year-olds concentrate far better when they are on the move or are confident that they can move if they wish.

When you watch young children (and some in the examples are rising threes), you will notice how much concentration they pour into chosen physical activities. They are ready and willing to try different ways to achieve their aim and confident two-year-olds will have a good try before they ask for help. The very fact that they can ask for help - given in those settings with an encouraging atmosphere - seems to help young children to make efforts that are impressive from the perspective of their current skills.

For example

- In Poplar Play, Chloe (two years old) carried a doll out into the garden. An early years practitioner offered her a small wheeled trolley for her doll. Chloe picked up a pillow. She saw me looking and informed me, 'That's her pillow'. Chloe spent time settling her doll into the buggy with the pillow. It was not easy because Chloe was still holding onto the doll and trying to get the pillow positioned to her satisfaction. After several attempts she was happy and set off round the square of path in the garden. Chloe trundled the wheeled trolley around part of the path and showed a practitioner her doll. The practitioner looked carefully and commented, 'You've got your dolly and her pillow'.
- At the same time Jerome (two years old) was working hard to manage a fair sized trolley with a long handle. This was not an easy task for Jerome, who was quite small in relation to his chosen trolley. The square path in the centre garden had right angle corners and, in one corner, a wooden post supporting the veranda roof. It took Jerome several goes to manoeuvre his trolley around this corner. But he persevered with a serious face of concentration (not at all unhappy), using the trolley handle to work it a short distance back and forth until he got the trolley completely round the corner. Jerome headed along the straight and then worked a similar movement on the other corners of the square path, without the additional block of the post.

For example

Active involvement in their own care and routines is an ideal way for three-year-olds to practise and apply skills.

- During my morning visit to Burnwood Nursery school in Staffordshire I could see how the children were active in Nursery routines. The school had a self-registration system at the beginning of the day or session and a self-service drink and snack time. Children had help whenever they wanted but they were enabled to organise their own part in nursery life.
- I was observing a three-year-old at the drinks table and inadvertently caught her eye. She looked at me and smiled while continuing to pour out her drink from the jug, missing her beaker. I noticed and, at the expression on my face, she looked down and righted the jug. There was a spill on the table but the early years practitioner close by was calm and uncritical. She gave the child some paper towel sheets and the child mopped up the table without any distress. The approach was that of 'accidents happen sometimes' and children were competent to right the situation.

For example

In Poplar Play, Michael (two years), Alric (three) and Charlotte (three) were all at a table with a special kind of jigsaw. The materials comprised a person in separate body parts that could be fitted together like a jigsaw. Then bits of material could be chosen and laid across to create clothes. A top flap was then brought down and the image created of a dressed person.

The group of four children focused on this activity. Charlotte did the actions but they all seemed to be contributing to the choosing of materials. They tried several different combinations of the small swatches of material to create different outfits for the jigsaw person.

Kayleigh, Marcella and Simone (all five-year-olds) enjoyed this activity slightly later in the afternoon. Watching them, it was noticeable that these older children were more able than the threes to line up the material straight across the completed figure. They were also able to smooth the material down so that the flap could shut more tightly. The enjoyment level looked very similar between the three-year-old small group and that of the five-year-olds, but the latter group showed more dexterity with their fine skills.

Rising threes and three-year-olds need plenty of space, indoors and outside, so that they can move. They need plenty of scope for practice.

- Three-year-olds and rising threes vary in physical skills, confidence and awareness of the feedback of their own bodies. It is not unusual that they still bump into people or furniture, especially if they are absorbed in a task. Yet if three-year-olds are focused on an activity then they can be very detailed in their movements.

- Sometimes, three-year-olds look 'clumsy' compared with older children. They can find it hard to change direction or stop, especially when moving at speed or to allow for other bodies close by them. Three-year-olds can handle simple games props but the careful looking and body co-ordination required for kicking a ball or hitting with a bat is beyond the ability of most three-year-olds.

- They can copy simple sequences of movement and often enjoy this kind of game, perhaps to music or song. Three-year-olds can have gained some of the finer movements of co-ordination, shown through their self-care and helping out in the daily routines. Their enjoyment of art and craft activities also highlights their ability to direct and control movement.

- Rising threes and three-year-olds are very likely to struggle with tools like scissors and need careful, unhurried practice with eating utensils or woodwork tools. The adjusting of jigsaws is still hard for some three-year-olds. They need lots of practice.

- The large movements are as important as the fine ones. Unfortunately, some adults greet large physical activity with much more 'Stop it!' and 'Calm down!' than the more valued small muscle co-ordination required for painting or writing.

- Three-year-olds have a range of large physical skills: lifting, carrying, climbing, running and jumping. Rising threes and the younger three-year-olds may still be struggling with some co-ordinations, such as how they launch off to jump with both feet at the time.

Being a helpful adult

Adults need to look with a fresh eye at what seem to be ordinary personal care routines.

- All the self-care skills require physical dexterity and hand eye co-ordination. Some personal routines need a grasp of order and sequence. For instance that you put your pants on before your trousers.
- Children are helped and can relax when adult words and actions communicate that they appreciate and value these learning tasks. You need to give time and quietly celebrate children's achievements with your words and smile.
- Self-care skills, much like use of tools, sometimes need to be broken down into the separate steps that make up the whole task. Helpful adults can share a sequence of 'first you... and then you..' but also can sometimes use useful techniques.
- Adults often underestimate the importance of practice in self-care skills. Children need to have relaxed practice to improve their skills and also the pleasure of showing that now a task is 'easy peasey'. They deserve having an adult show appreciation, rather than any sense that at three years old, or any other age, the child 'should' be able to manage this skill. Such a mean-spirited approach is discouraging for children.

- Three-year-olds have improved balance, although some are still wobbly. They may be able to stand on tip toe, which is hard until they master the different balance involved.

- Three-year-olds can be confident in riding three-wheeled bikes. But it is worth recognising that bike riding is a cluster of skills that take practice and concentration. Children have to work out how to get on and off bikes, how to make the pedals go in a steady forward action, how to steer and how to stop.

- Three-year-olds playing with friends often use their physical skills in construction and pretend play games. These young children often struggle on joint activities. It is one thing to work out how you alone carry boxes or bricks in order to make a construction or help in tidying up large items. It is a different set of co-ordinations and communication skills to carry a large item with your friends and manoeuvre it into place.

- Many of the three-year-old physical skills are shown through their self-care (see also page 19). The usual tasks of dressing, eating and managing in the toilet are complex sequences of actions that young children need to learn and to have relaxed time to practise. Their growing sense of competence supports feelings of confidence and self-worth and should not be underestimated within an early years curriculum.

For example

In Poplar Play, Charlotte (three years) was working on some constructional materials at a nearby table. She used careful looking and touch to line up the pieces of wood (that have holes in them) for a wooden nail or screw shape. Charlotte hammered with care and concentration. She seemed to enjoy showing me what she had done at each stage. Finally, she completed a structure with three 'arms' that were movable on a 'nail' and told me, 'It's a clock'.

For example

In New River Green, Rosie (three years) showed her fine physical skills through what she chose to make, but her play also highlighted her current interests. In the first part of the morning, Rosie was at the dough table with three other children. She was working on her batch of dough and said to the practitioner, 'It's a hiding place'. The practitioner asked, 'What's going to hide in it?' and Rosie said, 'A baby's going to hide'.

Later in the morning, when Rosie was doing a jigsaw with me, she extracted a carefully folded piece of paper from her pocket and said, 'Close your eyes'. She placed it in my outstretched hand. She had a small piece of paper coloured pink, with an even smaller piece fixed to the middle. Rosie explained, 'It's a hiding place'.

Understanding about their own bodies

Three-year-olds are likely to understand some aspects of bodies and health but it will be a very individual pattern, reflecting their experience.

For example

- Three-year-olds are interested to learn about bodies and health but in ways that relate to what makes sense to them. Young children ask questions, share experiences and show their current knowledge with interested adults.

- At three years old Georgia (described by Cath Arnold) showed her special knowledge about health that she had learned because of the allergic condition of her baby brother Harry. She explained to her grandmother, 'Have a small cake for Harry 'cos he's not allowed eggs and chocolate'. She saw her father looking closely at a pot of fromage frais and asked, 'You are looking to see if Harry's allowed that? You looking at ingredients?'.

- At New River Green, Rosie rubbed her head at one point and I asked, 'Have you had a bang?' Rosie said confidently, 'No' and then informed me, 'If the sun comes out you get a headache. If somebody bangs you, you get a headache.'

- Three-year-olds are closely interested in minor injury and consolation. In Poplar Play Centre, Michael (two years) had slightly hurt his finger. He showed the finger to a practitioner who expressed sympathy, 'Did you hurt your finger? How did you do that?' Chloe (two years) and a second girl were close by and they moved in to see and listen. Later when we were sitting inside, Charlotte (three years) showed me a scrape (very minor) on her leg and Alric (also three years) pulled up his trouser leg to show me his scrape (almost invisible) as well. None of the children wanted massive amounts of attention. The examples are a reminder that for three-year-olds what happens to their own body, and that of their friends, is of great interest.

For example

At New River Green there was a lot of conversation revolving around the dough table as children arrived and wanted to chat. The practitioner managed the beginnings and ends of the different conversation, often on very different topics, depending on what the children wanted to tell her. It varied from what they were doing with the dough, to a discussion about snoring (see below), Winnie the Pooh and details of Bob the Builder. The snoring conversation highlighted how children can be interested in all kinds of everyday events.

James (three years) wanted to tell the practitioner about last night. 'I were snoring', he announced with a grin. The practitioner asked, 'Who told you that you were snoring?' James explained, 'My Mummy. Sometimes I snore.' James asked a question that I could not hear that must have been about why or when people snore, because the practitioner explained, 'People only snore when they're asleep'. James laughed and claimed, 'My Mummy's snoring today' and the practitioner laughed in reply, saying, 'Is she having a sleep?'

For example

An entertaining physical game in Poplar Play showed not only the physical skills of some children but their awareness of their peers.

Chloe (two years old), Charlotte (three years old) and Kayleigh (five years old) were busy working the four-seater rocker. The rocker was on a spring and the girls were competent in making the equipment move in deep dives and back up again. Two other children, Alric (three years old) and Jack (two and a half) had tried and found the vigorous rocking a bit strong for their taste. But the girls had swiftly stopped the rocking to let each boy get off without complaining. Kayleigh had the longest legs and used her body to steady the rocker on some occasions. As the youngest and smallest, Chloe slipped a bit from a firm seating once or twice and the other girls slowed to let her re-position herself.

Isobelle (not quite two years) was interested to watch the rocking group and steadily moved closer. The girls watched her warily and were slowing their vigorous rocking motion as I moved across and guided Isobelle back a couple of paces. Kayleigh and Charlotte looked pleased as Isobelle moved back with me and nodded, 'Because she's little'.

Creative Development

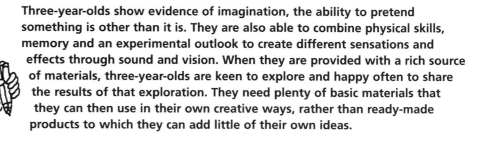

Three-year-olds show evidence of imagination, the ability to pretend something is other than it is. They are also able to combine physical skills, memory and an experimental outlook to create different sensations and effects through sound and vision. When they are provided with a rich source of materials, three-year-olds are keen to explore and happy often to share the results of that exploration. They need plenty of basic materials that they can then use in their own creative ways, rather than ready-made products to which they can add little of their own ideas.

Three-year-olds are also learning attitudes, so they can already show signs of wanting to produce the picture that an adult wants or waiting to be shown what they should stick and where in their collage. Three-year-olds are learning considerably more than techniques and tool use. First-hand, direct experiences promote creativity in young children. Three-year-olds need a wide range of opportunities to be actively engaged. When children's interest and curiosity is engaged, then they want to represent what they have seen and heard: through art and craft, imaginative play and recounting what was of interest to them.

On the other hand, three-year-olds who are regularly directed and told what to do in so-called 'creative activities' will learn one of two broad outlooks. Some children will learn that adults decide what is worthwhile and that the three- and four-year-old task is to find out what adults want and to produce it with the minimum of fuss and challenge. Other children will decide the adult-driven activity is boring, will stay put for the least time tolerated and then go off to do something much more interesting, and possibly more genuinely supportive of their learning. Unreflective adults may then claim that these children 'have no concentration' or 'will have to be made to do their work'.

For example

At the woodwork table in New River Green, three-year-olds, showed impressive powers of concentration, and they were allowed to take as much time as needed. These young children persevered with their saw, not an easy tool until you get the right technique. I watched several three-year-olds continue to work away, appreciating discreet adult guidance about the best way to saw, until they had sawed off their piece of work. Then they either took a breather, with their wood named and put safely on a shelf or took it straight to another table for choices about hammering in nails, or painting.

Three-year-olds can have and be further developing:

- An enthusiasm for creation in art and craft materials. They make choices about materials they want and judgements about whether they are happy with what they have done so far or the finished product.

- Three-year-olds often want to explore variations around a theme. They may have become interested in swirls, a stripes effect or what happens if they fold paper. They are often interested to learn other ways of making interesting effects but still need to have chances to practise and explore in their own ways. Three-year-olds in a relaxed activity are intrigued to explore what materials can do.

- They apply their fine physical movements with careful and attentive looking as they use woodwork tools, build, work the playdough and create painting and collage.

- Three-year-olds usually enjoy songs and singing. They show their powers of recognition and recall, not only in small group singing time but also in the spontaneous singing that happy children start at any time.

- Three-year-olds are often tuneful and this skill demonstrates their control of their language: not just the words but also the varying volume of some songs, rhythm and emotional tone. They are also tuneful in their created songs and self-talk when playing. Three-year-olds sometimes play with words, repeated phrases and tone. Not all three-years-olds are enthusiastic singers, but many show high levels of enjoyment.

- Three-year-olds can be adept music makers, with simple musical instruments that enable them to keep time and rhythm. A few three-year-olds may manage to dance at the same time but this double co-ordination can be tricky.

- Some three-year-olds already want to sing, dance or recount a story in front of a small familiar group and it is appropriate to provide the opportunity. Some three-year-olds, as well as fours and fives, are not happy performers. It is unwise to insist and push a child into doing something in front of a group. This usually creates an unhappy experience that in no way encourages effort in the future.

Food for thought

Music is the area of creative expression in which early years practitioners and parents sometimes lack confidence. There is not usually the same level of unease as with maths, but some adults can feel, 'My singing is so out of tune' or 'If only I could play a proper musical instrument.'

Young children do not make these harsh judgements. They are happy that familiar adults sing to them from the earliest months. They like music and as toddlers soon join in any kind of music making and they love dancing. At no point do they require that their familiar adults are public performance standard on any of these creative skills.

- Three-year-olds are keen to look and listen. They can already express preferences about pictures they like and music they prefer. Three-year-olds who have experienced a range of kinds of music can make choices as well as understand that perhaps a piece of music that 'sounds like the waves' is their music for the restful period after lunch.

Children will vary a great deal in this area depending on their experience. Some three-year-olds and rising threes will have plenty of experience of creative activities from nursery, family or childminder's home, others may have next to no experience, especially of the creative activities that generate more of what adults call 'mess'. A similar gap may be observable for dancing, music, songs and rhymes. Some three-year-olds will have had a wide range of experience from being a baby and toddler. Some rising threes who enter an early years setting may already know or recognise a range of songs and know the hand movements well. Some of their peers will have far more limited experience and the activities to support creative development within the Foundation Stage may be a fresh experience for them.

For example

Many young children enjoy the pleasure of dancing: the freedom of movement as well as choosing to follow the rhythm and pace of a particular piece of music.

- Three-year-olds often enjoy free dance sessions. I have seen some lively and much enjoyed dance times in nurseries, when adults join in as well. Rising threes and some two-year-olds can move rhythmically and enjoy their own dancing as well as sometimes dancing with adults.

- Some three- and four-year-olds have an impressive sense of rhythm and are especially well able to follow a beat, even to keep in time with each other. In a nursery I used to visit in the east end of London, a small group of three- and four-year-old boys had drawn impressive glances during a visit to the local market. Hearing the music from one of the stalls, they had spontaneously shifted into a rhythmic dance in tune with the music and each other, as they moved along the street.

For example

Children are interested to explore different kinds of materials. In Poplar Play, Charlotte (three years old) and Kayleigh (five years old) were equally interested to sit at the table with flat trays filled with a thick, pink mixture.

They both understood about putting on the overalls before sitting down and did not need any reminding. Kayleigh was able to do it herself and Charlotte asked me for help. The overalls were a more difficult physical task for a three-year-old, since they fitted on arms in first and with a Velcro fixing at the back of the child's neck.

I asked what the pink material in the trays was, and Kayleigh explained, 'It's cornflour'. Both girls were keen to explore the mixture and concentrated on using the available tools, including metal spoons and wooden spatulas. Charlotte liked to feel and smooth the mixture with her fingers. Some of the mixture got onto her fingertips and she worked it off with care, finger by finger. She used the spoon to scrape and watched the mixture dribble thickly back on the tray. Kayleigh was more interested in using the spoon to scrape and carve patterns, then smoothing it out.

Charlotte's interest in removing the cornflour mix from her fingers reminded me of an activity described to me, but not observed myself. A group of rising threes and three-year-olds in a nursery had a grand time with glue and spreaders. They did not want to stick anything on that day but were fascinated by how the glue could be swept and swished around on the table by a nifty wrist action with the spreader. They then explored spreading the glue on their fingers. The glue dried quickly and this group of young children had a highly focused time peeling the dried glue off one finger after another.

For example

As with almost any kind of activity in which children are engaged, a primarily creative activity will bring in other areas of learning for the child, and insights if you are watching and listening as an attentive adult.

In New River Green, Rosie (three years) was keen to do a painting on the easel set up under the outdoor covered veranda. She beckoned me over to explain and show that she could not do a painting because the paper would not stay flat. Rosie pointed to the single bulldog clip in the centre saying, 'I can't do it'. She demonstrated how the edges of the thick paper kept rolling inwards, as fast as she tried to flatten them. I suggested, 'Do you think we need more clips?' Rosie looked closely at the easel and commented, 'We need clips. We need one, two. We need two more.' She pointed to the location as she said each counting word.

We went off together and asked a practitioner for clips. Fixing them was tricky for three-year-old fingers. So Rosie showed where each clip should be located, I hooked them over the easel and she pushed them well down. Then she took up her brush.

Very soon Ben (four years) came to join Rosie. They painted peaceably together, each working with one half of the paper. Rosie looked at their joint painting and at Ben and said, 'We're friends aren't we?'. The comment seemed to relate to the fact that they could share the same piece of paper and paint. When their joint painting was complete, Rosie and Ben went off together to play with the small world farm that was in another part of the garden.

Another aspect of creativity is a problem-solving experimental outlook. With familiar materials, three-year-olds will sometimes show an open mindedness to try different ways to make something work. Often three-year-olds need a hint or two from helpful adults to support problem-solving. Young children tend to see the situation as it is at the moment and not how it might be, with some changes. With your help and friendly conversation, three-year-olds can gather the experience to support an outlook that says 'Maybe we could change this...' or 'What if we did that...?' Three-year-olds can show technological creativity when they are given a rich resource of materials, many of which will be recycled. Young children especially relish the problem-solving possibilities of many outdoor activities. Interesting and practical problems can be faced with 'How are we going to move all this earth from here to there? or 'How do we fix the covers on our den?' Access to space, time, natural materials and the chance to get a bit mucky are a real plus for many children.

Food for thought

I was struck as I looked through the examples I gathered for this book, just how much we can view spontaneous singing as an unobtrusive measure of children's happiness in a setting or home.

Unhappy children do not break into song as they work the rocker (example page 49), nor do they make up tuneful little ditties as they do a jigsaw (example on page 20). Children who feel under pressure do not create four-year-old choral harmonies as they tidy up the home corner (example in *What Does it Mean to be Four?* page 51) nor do they flow spontaneously into lengthy song and dance routines (example in *What Does it Mean to be Five?* page 54).

In the settings where I made these observations, the practitioners had shared songs and rhymes with the children in enjoyable small group sessions. But it was a credit to the positive social atmosphere, created by supportive adults, that the children viewed singing as part of life. The message from children's behaviour was that you broke into song when you felt content; it was another way of expressing yourself as a child.

Imagination and pretend play

Three-year-olds demonstrate their creativity and awareness of everyday life through their pretend play. Young children take what they know of familiar life and routines and then play around with it. Many three-year-olds will also have enough experience from stories, television or children's video and film to explore pure fantasy. When you listen and watch three-year-olds exercise their imagination you have a window onto how they think the world works, what is important and what is interesting these individual children. There is, of course, a great deal of variety between children in what they want to funnel through their pretend play but content three-year-olds will use their imagination in this way.

For example

I enjoyed listening and watching a long pretend play sequence in the block area of New River Green Centre between Rosie (three years) and Ben (four years), who spent quite a lot of time together at different parts of the day. The entire sequence lasted for close to half an hour and from the excerpts here it is possible to see how the two young children moved seamlessly from one theme to another. Two adults were close by: an early year practitioner sitting at a nearby table, sometimes with other children and Ben's mother who was staying in response to his request that she play with him a while before she left.

Ben and Rosie started by building a see-saw structure with blocks and a short plank. They sat on it but the see-saw motion was not successful. Ben said, 'But it won't go'. Rosie replied, 'I'll get a bigger one' and then 'I'm going to make my own'. She moved a slight distance to another part of the block and began to choose pieces of wood.

Rosie finished her own construction without needing any help and announced, 'I've made a bridge'. Ben told the practitioner with some concern, 'She's taking Jon's bricks (one of the boys who were being Bob the Builders earlier – see the example on page 26). The practitioner acknowledged Ben's concern with, 'That's all right. Jon is playing outside now. But that was a nice thought.'

Rosie and Ben worked close by each other in the block area, making their own personal constructions but talking together and looking as well. They confidently called for the attention of Ben's mother and the early years practitioner whenever they wanted direct admiration of their constructions so far. And at one point they stopped work to chat about the heavy rain that fell in the previous night. Both children returned smoothly to their constructions, switching attention between chatting, building, finding pieces of wood and chatting again.

By now Rosie and Ben had both made complex, long constructions using a range of hollow blocks and planks. Rosie announced, 'We can go under it', but looked dubious as she scanned the construction. The practitioner commented, 'Do you think it's big enough to go under?' - the children would not have been able to fit under or through bits of their constructions.

Ben now decided that his structure was a rocket and then that it was an 'astronaut'. He sounded confused between the two and his mother explained simply that the astronaut was the person and the rocket was what they travelled in. Rosie announced that her structure was 'a bridge'.

Then Ben said, 'There's a dragon. Quick! Get our swords.' Both children picked up short wooden planks, that they held before them like weapons. Rosie said, 'We're going to get their fire out' and she and Ben made a sound like rushing water. Rosie explained, ' Mine has got fire and water' and Ben said, 'Mine has got poo and pee and fire and water'.

Ben's mother said mildly, 'That sounds a bit smelly' and the practitioner commented with a smile, 'But it might sort out the dragon'. Rosie and Ben were then discussing sweets. It was unclear whether the dragons were after their pretend sweets or that it was okay for the dragons to eat the sweets.

Rosie returned to her structure to put her plank/water gun back into the space from which she had removed it. But one of the uprights had shifted and she had trouble balancing the plank on the two uprights. Rosie looked and could see that her bridge was not level any more and said, 'This is wrong'. Ben's mother explained that Rosie probably needed to move the upright. Ben's mother explained in simple words but did not move in to do the readjustment. Rosie juggled the upright until it sat more firmly and then placed the plank on top once more. She looked satisfied, watched by Ben's mother who wisely waited to see if Rosie did need help.

Rosie and Ben then pulled materials out of a basket that was available in the block area. They wanted to drape their constructions. Both children spontaneously named the colour of the cloth they were using and draped their own constructions with great care. Rosie was having more difficulty achieving the effect she wanted. Ben offered, 'Rosie, do you want me to help you. You can help with mine.' But Rosie replied, 'I want to do it.' Ben announced, 'This is going to be lovely and blue and black'.

After some more struggle, Rosie now said, 'I can't put this on properly'. The practitioner offered, 'Do you want some help?' and moved closer as Rosie nodded. The practitioner then asked, 'How do you want it done?' Rosie explained, 'All over the blocks'. The practitioner draped the cloth in the way indicated by Rosie's arm gestures and she was happy with the result.

Rosie and Ben now chose to create the scenario of having lunch. The children selected different sized blocks to represent the food they needed and explained that they were laying out the food on the tables. Rosie said, 'I've got everything I need' and Ben explained, 'We need to cut the food'. Rosie giggled and said, 'Silly billy - I forgot.' Ben took up a plank and said, 'It's our measurer'. Rosie looked at the plank and suggested, 'This could be our.. our .. our to shoot the very scary dinosaur'. Ben appeared to mishear and said with some concern, 'You don't shoot fairies'. Rosie repeated her idea with, 'A very very scary dinosaur'. Ben still thought Rosie was talking about shooting fairies and his mother explained, 'No, she said very very scary. A dinosaur'.

Note: In this pretend play sequence, the children's fantasy was allowed to run, including the short excursions into pretend weaponry. The team at New River Green has discussed at length the question of super hero play and related weaponry. Like a number of other thoughtful early years teams, they have changed their practice from stopping this kind of play to allowing the pretend play to evolve, unless there are genuine issues about rough or aggressive behaviour. I think this whole sequence shows that such an approach is wiser than heavy-handed adult intervention. This issue is also discussed in *What Does it Mean to be Four?* on page 52.

What should concern you?

There is great variety within the three-year-old age range and some children will be more at ease or enthusiastic than their peers.

- It would be appropriate to be concerned about children who show a serious lack of social skills, with difficulty in relating to other children even when they have had time to settle and you have observed them in quiet, apparently relaxed situations. Some children, who are later found to have some level of autistic spectrum disorder, are often noticed as three-year-olds whose development already contrasts with their peers. Children may show confusion in relations with other children, are anxious about the most minor changes of routine and perplexed by the kind of play, especially pretend play, that most three-year-olds can manage.

- Perhaps children appear to be insecure, despite plenty of reassurance and are highly anxious about new challenges, even minor ones. Some three-year-olds have already taken on adult, perhaps parents', anxiety about not making mistakes, doing high quality 'work' and producing something by the end of each day.

- Three-year-olds vary considerably and some are quiet. You should, however, be concerned, about three-year-olds who have settled with you and have limited language. It should be possible for you to understand what three-year-olds say, perhaps with a little tuning-in time. Three-year-olds should be able to understand what you say in appropriate words and phrases for this age group. It is, of course, a different matter if you and the child do not share the same fluent language.

- There may be a number of reasons for a child's struggles with communication. You would need to explore those in partnership with the child's parents. Possibilities could be some level of hearing loss, or intermittent deafness, that has not yet been identified. There are a range of learning disabilities that affect children's ability to communicate, some of which can be hard to identify.

- Three-year-olds vary considerably in terms of physical skills and some will have more obvious confidence or co-ordination than others. You would be right to be concerned about any children with significant problems of balance and co-ordination in comparison with their peers. Undiagnosed problems with vision or hearing difficulties that affect balance might be an issue. Clearly you would talk with parents as well as make some careful observations of children, seeing whether some kinds of movement are harder than others.

- Three-year-olds are naturally lively, need to move and can be restless and unhappy if forced into sedentary activities. Sometimes you may need to address the unrealistic expectations of other adults: colleagues or parents. Some young children who have ADHD may be noticeable at three years of age because their struggles to attend and stay still are so different from their more normally active peers. But far more often you will need to give reassurance that wanting to run and jump and shout is normal three-year-old behaviour.

Further reading and resources

- Caddell, Dorothy *Numeracy Counts* (Scottish Consultative Council on the Curriculum* 1998)

- Caddell, Dorothy *Numeracy in the Early Years: What the Research Tells us* (Scottish Consultative Council on the Curriculum* 1998)

- Caddell, Dorothy *Working with Parents: a Shared Understanding of the Curriculum 3-5* (Learning and Teaching Scotland 2001) (Tel: 01382 443600, website www.LTScotland.com)

- Campbell, Robin *Literacy from Home to School: Reading with Alice* (Trentham Books 1999)

- Clark, Alison and Moss, Peter *Listening to Young Children: the Mosaic Approach* (National Children's Bureau 2001)

- Collins, Margaret *Because We're Worth it: Enhancing Self-esteem in Young Children* and *Circle Time for the Very Young* (Lucky Duck Publishing 2001 Tel: 0117 973 2881)

- DATEC: Iram Siraj-Blatchford and John Siraj-Blatchford lead this very practical project (Developmentally Appropriate Technology for Early Childhood). You can access the reports and useful guidance on the website www.ioe.ac.uk

- Duffy, Bernadette *Supporting Creativity and Imagination in the Early Years* (Open University Press 1998)

- Finch, Sue *'An Eye for an Eye Leaves Everyone Blind': Teaching Young Children to Settle Conflicts without Violence* (National Early Years Network** 1998)

- Greig, Liz *Supporting Development and Learning: 3-5* (Learning and Teaching Scotland 2001)

- Goddard Blythe, Sally Articles available from the Institute of Neuro-Physiological Psychology (Tel: 01244 311414, website www.inpp.org.uk)

- Hancock, Juliet and Dale, Barbara *Looking, Listening and Learning: Quality Interaction with Children* (Scottish Consultative Council on the Curriculum* 2000)

- Healy, Jane *Your Child's Growing Mind* (Doubleday 1994)

- Healy, Jane *Failure to Connect: How Computers Affect Our Children's Minds and What We Can Do About It* (Simon and Schuster 1998)

- Hughes, Anne and Ellis, Sue *Writing it Right? Children Writing 3-8* (Scottish Consultative Council on the Curriculum* 1998)

- Lindon, Jennie *Understanding Child Development: Knowledge, Theory and Practice* (Thomson Learning 1998)

- Lindon, Jennie *Equal Opportunities in Practice* (Hodder and Stoughton 1998)

- Lindon, Jennie *Understanding World Religions in Early Years Practice* (Hodder and Stoughton 1999)

- Lindon, Jennie *Too Safe for their own Good? Helping Children Learn about Risk and Life Skills* (National Early Years Network** 1999)

- Lindon, Jennie *Helping Babies and Toddlers Learn: a Guide to Good Practice with Under Threes* (National Early Years Network** 2000)

- Lindon, Jennie *Understanding Children's Play* (Nelson Thornes 2001)

- Lindon, Jennie *Child Care and Early Education: Good Practice to Support Young Children and their Families* (Thomson Learning 2002)

- Miller, Judy *Never too Young: How Young Children can Take Responsibility and Make Decisions - a Handbook for Early Years Workers* (National Early Years Network** 1996)

- Ouvry, Marjorie *Exercising Muscles and Minds: Outdoor Play and the Early Years Curriculum* (National Early Years Network** 2000)

- Qualifications and Curriculum Authority *Curriculum Guidance for the Foundation Stage* (2000)

- Qualifications and Curriculum Authority and DfEE *Planning for Learning in the Foundation Stage* (2001)

- Perkins, Sam *Seeing, Making, Doing: Creative Development in Early Years Settings* (National Early Years Network** 1998)

- Roberts, Rosemary *Self-esteem and Early Learning* (Paul Chapman 2002)

- Save the Children project: Lina Fajerman, Michael Jarrett and Faye Sutton *Children as Partners in Planning: a Training Resource to Support Consultation with Children*

- Wilkinson, Gay *The Early Learning Goals in Practice* (Step Forward Publishing 2000)

* SCCC titles are now available from Learning and Teaching Scotland (Tel: 01382 443600, Website www.LTScotland.com

** All NEYN titles are available from the National Children's Bureau (Tel: 020 7843 6000)

Videos

- *The High/Scope Approach for Under Threes* High/Scope UK Tel: 020 8676 0220

- *Tuning into Children* Book and video from National Children's Bureau

- *Learning Together with Threes* and *Learning Together with Fours* from the PEEP Centre, Peers School, Littlemore, Oxford OX4 6JZ Tel: 01865 779779

Acknowledgements

I have learned a great deal through discussions with early years practitioners and consultants and through visits to a wide range of early years settings. In connection with this book, I would especially like to thank the staff team and children at:

- Brighton and Hove Playlink - home visiting and drop in scheme
- Burnwood Nursery School in Staffordshire
- New River Green Early Years Centre and Family Project (referred to in brief within the book as New River Green), North London
- Poplar Play Centre (referred to in brief within the book as Poplar Play), East London
- Saplings Nursery in South London
- St Peter's Eaton Square CE Primary School nursery class (referred to in brief within the book as St Peter's).

I would like to thank the following individuals whose ideas on early years practice have been so valuable:

- Jean Ainsworth-Smith (Head of St Peter's Eaton Square CE Primary School nursery class)
- Cherry Baker (Deputy Head of Windham Nursery within Windham Early Excellence Centre)
- Jacqui Cousins (early years consultant)
- Dymphna Dale (Manager of Poplar Play Centre)
- Annie Davy (Oxford EYDCP)
- Margaret Edgington (early years consultant)
- Kevin Kelman (deputy head and early years author)
- Anita Mohindra (Head of New River Green Early Years Centre and Family Project)
- Stephanie Moran (Education Department, Stoke-on-Trent)
- Alice Sharp (Early Years Executive, Scottish Independent Nurseries Association)
- Iram Siraj-Blatchford (Professor of Early Childhood Education, Institute of Education)
- Penny Tassoni (early years consultant)
- Sylvia Wilkinson (Brighton and Hove Playlink Project Officer)

I have changed the names of most of the children in the examples. The exceptions are:

- Drew and Tanith, who are my own (now adult) son and daughter and have given their permission for me to use the descriptive diaries I kept of them both in their early years.
- Georgia is the child described by Cath Arnold in her book *Child Development and Learning 2-5 Years: Georgia's Story* (Paul Chapman Publishing, 1999). Georgia's individual development is described from the diary that her family kept as well as the material from the time that she attended Pen Green Early Years Centre.
- Alice is the granddaughter of Robin Campbell who describes her early development in *Literacy from Home to School: Reading with Alice* (Trentham Books, 1999).